The Real Estate Broker's

Inside Guide to Selling

Your Own Home

The Real Estate Broker's Inside Guide to Selling Your Own Home

(*And Keeping the Commission!*)

ALEXANDER MASON

Coward, McCann & Geoghegan
NEW YORK

Library of Congress Cataloging in Publication Data

Mason, Alexander, date.
    The real estate broker's inside guide to selling
your own home (and keeping the commission!)

    1. House selling.   I. Title.
HD1379.M397 1982   333.33′8   82-7307
ISBN 0-698-11138-9   AACR2

Contents

1

Sell It Yourself

If you are like most people in the United States, your home is the most valuable possession you own. And during the past decade of inflation you have seen the dollar value of your home more than double to a figure that you never thought possible. Without doing anything, you have become rich—on paper, anyway. This might be the time to sell.

During my many years as a real estate broker I have found that the decision to sell a home has little to do with taking a profit. People sell a house because the family has grown and now the house is too small, because the family has shrunk and now the house is too large, because the job takes them to another place, because they want a more luxurious house or want to move to an apartment in the city—there are almost as many reasons as sales. And if you bought your house ten years or more before now, you will make a profit.

Because of this profit you should think about the tax considerations before you make a final decision. The Tax Reform Act of 1978 allows you to take a profit of up to $100,000 on the sale of your house without paying capital gains tax if you're fifty-five years old or over—just once in your lifetime. If you're under fifty-five, you'll have to reinvest any profit in another home sometime during the year to avoid paying tax.

If you have decided to sell, then you know that the big boom market in housing is just about over. Between high prices and high interest rates most Americans have been priced out of the market—creating a situation where there are many sellers and few buyers. Although at this time, both mortgage rates and prices seem to be easing, I have never seen such a sluggish market and it may still not be an easy job to sell your house.

In a boom market, a mere advertisement might bring a buyer. And whether in a boom or bust, the easiest way to sell your house is always through someone like me—a professional real estate broker. I earn fees because of my inside knowledge about the market, and the options that sellers and buyers have at their disposal. I also have access to the greatest number of buyers.

But, with some time and work, and the benefit of my inside information about current real estate practices, you could sell your own home and save thousands of dollars in broker's commissions. You then have a negotiating buffer—you can keep this commission for yourself (you will *work* for it), or if the real estate market is slow in your area, you can reduce the price of your house to attract buyers without taking a loss.

The Best Time to Sell

When is the best time to sell? Properties always show better in the spring and summer. It has been said, "If you like the house when the snow is on the ground, you'll love it when the sun is in the sky." I have found as a general rule that the best selling season is in the spring or early summer.

When Should You Give Possession?

This is a critical question, particularly when children of school age are involved. Generally speaking, a closing could take from thirty to ninety days. However, it could be extended to the end of school, which might be a longer period.

An important rule to follow is never to permit a buyer to move into the house until formal transfer of the property has taken place. Even though you may have to move before the closing, it is safer to leave the property vacant. Possession is nine-tenths of the law. If anything unforeseen should happen and the sale is not consummated, you would have the expense and annoyance of getting the people out.

Financing

If you are going to do my job—sell a house—you must know about financing. The single most important feature of a house for today's homebuyer is not the playroom or the kitchen or how many bedrooms or baths there are, but—what are the financing options? Creative financing is the catchword in real estate today. You must also know how to prepare your home for sale, how to advertise and show it, how to close the sale.

The information contained in this book is the result of thousands of hours of dealing with real estate problems—and both buyers and sellers. You are gaining access to knowledge gleaned from making millions of dollars of sales in real estate. Learn some of the techniques, work on selling your own house, and when you have finished, you will have a sense of satisfaction that will only be exceeded by being thousands of dollars richer.

2

Setting a Price
on Your House

Never, never ask a friend, unless that friend happens to be a professional real estate broker, "What price should I put on my house?"

If your friends volunteer a price, try asking: "Will you—or do you know of anyone who would be ready, willing, and able to—buy my house at the price you are suggesting?"

It's easy to get off on the wrong foot the minute you start thinking about what your house is worth. Here's a typical example, from my own experience, that every real estate broker is familiar with. Mrs. Anderson decided to sell her house. She called my real estate office and asked for a price evaluation.

My procedure is to send two or three knowledgeable brokers to the house for a physical inspection. But before I do this, I consult the records on comparable sales to use as a guide for the inspection. After a thorough investigation, I compare notes with the other agents. We decided, in this case, that a price of $120,000 should sell the house within a thirty-day period, allowing for 5 percent negotiation.

When we presented our recommendations to Mrs. Anderson she flew into a rage: "You don't have the slightest idea what you're doing! You're all trying to steal my house! I've never been so insulted. My friend warned me not to take a penny less than $160,000."

Mrs. Anderson (a fictitious name in this case) practically threw me through her very expensive front door. A few days later, the house came on the market for $160,000.

Epilogue. Two years later, Mrs. Anderson's house finally sold for $105,000. Not only had we been within the parameters of what the house eventually sold for, but Mrs. Anderson—by overpricing—had to support two more years of mortgage payments, interest, and taxes.

Emotional involvement can be an enormous barrier to setting a realistic price on a house. If you cannot tolerate the frustration of showing your house and negotiating deals that sometimes fall through, you may set a price that is too low. In that case you'll regret it later and continue to feel that you cheated yourself.

On the other hand, when you hear of friends and neighbors making a killing in real estate ("Jack paid twenty thou for his house five years ago and he just sold it for $200,000—and it's not half the house mine is!"), you can work yourself into an unrealistic price range.

Once you have decided to sell, you must make every attempt to be objective—about the present real estate market, the location of your house, the house itself, and your own financial picture.

Evaluating the Price

What is the level of real estate in your area? Does the price you want seem to conform to that of other houses in the vicinity?

The neighborhood itself is of intrinsic value, and this value is part of the house price. Contiguous-land uses also have a lot to do with the value of a house and lot. If the land next door to your house is highly desirable, it increases the value of your house as well. A small house on a small lot in a suburban community may go for an unusually high price if that house is surrounded by a much larger piece of land that is likely to retain its rural quality. These little houses are sometimes called "estate quality." If your house and lot borders on, say, a state park or large estate, your house may command a much higher price than similar houses and lots in the same community.

The views from a house can also increase its value and its desirability. This is true of lakeside cottages as well as city co-ops. Although a view is not actually a physical attribute, it can be more important than the physical setting of the house. A house that has the potential of good views but fails to take advantage of them is a constant frustration to its owner. And a house that exploits the possible surrounding views is a source of continual pleasure to those who live in it. And that quality can be translated into dollar value.

Appliances, lighting fixtures, expensive finishes on floors and walls, can also make an enormous difference in the price—and future value—of a house.

All of these things should be taken into consideration when you determine the asking price of your house. And the question is double-edged: will these attributes be worth money to a buyer personally? And can you use them as selling points? If the attributes of a house add to its future value, they can be worth money to you immediately by incorporating them into your asking price.

Whether or not a house appreciates in value relates directly to what we in the real estate business refer to as "performance." Performance, to a realtor, means how a house functions—maintenance, repairs, energy, and so on; the term "community" refers to all of the advantages and disadvantages of the neighborhood.

15

Every house has advantages and disadvantages. But a disadvantage for one person may prove an advantage for another. One person's dream may be another's nightmare. Buyers always bring their own prejudices and their unique personal needs to a house.

If you are selling a house or co-op in the city, you will have different criteria. Some buyers will think a great, spacious co-op in an unfashionable part of town is a good trade-off and will pay for it. Others will buy a small, poorly lit space as long as it's on a good street. Define the advantages of your house or apartment and emphasize them as selling points. Also evaluate noise levels, building services, sunlight, security, transportation—all of these can add or subtract dollars from your asking price.

The Best Evaluation

To successfully evaluate a house, almost everyone should consult a professional appraiser. Real estate brokers are best qualified to give you a realistic market evaluation: the price your property will probably sell for within a reasonable time.

Although you might consider it unfair to call a broker for an evaluation when you are trying to sell your house yourself, this is one of the everyday routines of his or her business. There is also an advantage in having an evaluation by someone who is not involved in selling your house—you can expect the broker to be more objective because he has no personal stake in the property. And there is always the possibility that for his services the broker will get the listing if you fail to sell on your own.

An appraisal doesn't mean that you have to sell at that price, but it does mean that every element has been considered in an evaluation: tax records, comparison with similar properties, additional improvements, and so on.

The cost of a professional appraisal is small compared to the weight and credibility it adds to your effort to sell your house. It is to your advantage—and the buyer's—to get a professional appraisal. An appraiser does not have to be a real estate broker, although those of us in the business can usually supply an excellent evaluation. Other professional appraisers can be reached by calling the probate secretary to the county judge at the county courthouse. He or she can give you a list of recommended appraisers and their fee schedule.

For a small fee the FHA will also appraise your property. Application forms are available at banks, savings and loan institutions, and local FHA offices. The FHA appraisal is especially helpful if the buyer is applying for an FHA-guaranteed mortgage loan.

Your Financial Picture

Once you have received a professional opinion, you must then set two prices in your mind:

1. The price you will ask
2. The price you will take

In working out your asking price, start with the amount you want to end up with, say, $80,000. Then add the "extras" to this price. As the seller you will have certain closing costs. Closing costs are worked out in different ways, and who pays for what can be part of the negotiating process. But generally, consider these estimated costs:

You want to receive:	$80,000
Add: Attorney's fee	500
Survey	250
Title policy	250
Prorated real estate tax	500
	$81,500
Broker's commission (or yours to keep if you follow this book): 6%	4,800
Asking price	$86,300

Your asking price is no longer $80,000—it's $86,300. This is how we usually work out an asking price with a seller.

The next step is to fix your "taking" price, which is, in some ways, more difficult to assess. The price you will accept is almost always dependent on negotiated items.

An important bargaining point between the two prices could be the extras.

The refrigerator, stove, dishwasher, dryer, rugs, washing machine, dining room chandelier, are all negotiating points. Which go with the house? Which items are negotiable? The chandelier, for example, could be replaced by you with another fixture. Be sure that the fate of every item is spelled out in the contract. Many a deal has gone down the drain over a very inexpensive family heirloom.

These are your bargaining tools. If you find a buyer who will pay your asking price, and meets all the conditions of sale, consider yourself very lucky; more often than not you will have to settle for something less. Negotiate.

3

Why Some Houses Sell Faster Than Others

According to one real estate survey, a house was on the market in 1978 for less than thirty days before it sold; by 1979 it was taking from thirty to sixty days to sell, and in 1980 as long as two to five months (except for a period in the summer when interest rates dropped and it took only thirty to sixty days). From March to June of 1981, the average selling time was three to six months.

Regardless of the marketplace, some houses sell literally overnight. Sometimes it's a matter of luck and not even the most experienced realtor can figure it out. As some homeowners have found, if the house has special features that a buyer has been seeking, it's like hitting the jackpot. But certain features have sales appeal even in a slow market.

I recently sold a five-bedroom wood-shingled colonial. The major selling point of the house was its energy-saving features. The owner had installed two wood-burning stoves, an automatic flue damper on the furnace, and had added extra insulation where possible. We also set the price with a sluggish market in mind—$174,000 instead of the $180,000 that a better market might have brought. Because of this more realistic price, the house sold immediately, allowing the owner to take advantage of a move to a new house he had just built. He could add to his profit the money he saved on the quick move.

Fuel efficiency has unquestionably become a major consideration for people who now have to assume a burdensome mortgage. Offering a lot of space for the money does not necessarily sell a home anymore. Gas heat, insulation, and just enough room for the family are what seem to count today. People seldom talk anymore about buying the biggest house they can afford.

Other factors count, too. A seller in Long Island, New York, sold her three-bedroom ranch home in seven days for $75,000. She believes it had a lot to do with the amount of attention she had taken to decorate the interior. The living room, kitchen, and family room had been paneled, and wall-to-wall carpeting had been installed throughout the house. The yard was fenced and the grounds landscaped. Prospective buyers all commented on the completeness and beauty of the property, and it seemed especially desirable to families with young children. The young couple who bought the house chose it because they knew it was in perfect "move-in" condition.

The owners had also cut fuel bills by having insulation blown into the attic. They were also willing to leave all the major appliances.

A friend of mine who's a real estate agent in upstate New York sold a house in one day for more than a half-million dollars! She agrees that even in a slow market, special houses command immediate attention. The custom-designed contemporary house she sold had vertical cedar siding, a cut-stone swimming pool, doors two inches thick, skylights, and dramatic window walls. Even the doorknobs were custom-made. The buyer didn't blink at the $525,000 price tag.

Many successful sellers believe that having their home in spotlessly clean condition convinces buyers that it has been well maintained. Prospective buyers frequently comment on how very clean and well kept a house looks. One seller had repainted the interior, increased the insulation, and installed a new furnace. The site of the four-bedroom house on a quiet, horseshoe-shaped street appealed to buyers with young children. The Cape Cod house sold almost immediately for $157,000—only $2,000 below the original asking price.

Home sellers today should be aware that the appeal patterns in home buying seem to be shifting. More single people are buying houses than ever before. A large lot is not important to most unmarried people. Talk in the industry characterizes buyers as "more anxious to have a place closer to the amenities."

Newly married couples are also changing in their home needs. They are more interested these days in the proximity of the house to a highway or their jobs than in the extremities of the neighborhood. Some newlyweds will accept a house in poor condition in exchange for a cheaper price tag. They have more time and energy than they do dollars, and it makes sense to do the work themselves.

All of these factors will be involved when you set a price on your house. Consider them and analyze your home carefully.

Getting Your Selling Points Together

Before you know *how* to sell your house, you must carefully assess its bad qualities as well as its good points. Occasionally you can turn a fault into a virtue, but I find that it's better simply to acknowledge the fault (if you have to) and emphasize the virtues.

Where Is the House Situated?

A buyer will carefully consider the site. Shade, sun, slopes and gradients, drainage, access to the road—each of these factors can increase, or diminish, the appeal of a house. They are also part of the financial picture. A buyer looking for maintenance-free grounds will not place much value on gardens, landscaping that requires upkeep, or an overgrown lot begging for a hoe or lawnmower. One who looks forward to gardening will love it. Soil quality and drainage will be important to any potential buyer.

The private or public view of the grounds is another selling point that can be turned two ways. Some landscaping sets off a house for public view. In fact, some houses are built and landscaped specifically for show quality, and that has appeal for some buyers—and is a disadvantage for others. If your house is placed for public view from the road or sidewalk, is there any part of the grounds that can be closed off for privacy? Consider both the public and private aspects of a house and lot. If your house is situated for privacy, say so—appeal to those buyers who value seclusion. If it's a showplace, emphasize that selling point, but try to offer the potential for a private spot within the property.

What Is the Floor Plan Like?

The floor plan is the key to how livable a house is. Is there a separate side or back entrance? Does the traffic pattern let you reach various parts of the house without walking through the living room or bedrooms? Wherever it is located, the living room should have only one entrance (unless it has sliding doors to a garden or patio). That dead-end quality keeps the room from being used as a traffic corridor and eliminates wear and tear. Buyers will be conscious of the floor plan.

A kitchen that is central to the house appeals to most families today. Kitchen windows should face south, west, or east to receive the most light.

Older houses usually have the best and biggest bedrooms. A house with fewer, more spacious rooms usually has more appeal than one with several small, cell-like rooms.

Hidden Aspects

Although it's easy to see how the floor plan affects day-to-day living, other aspects of a house are more hidden. There are some things buyers cannot observe directly, but which they may ask about. And it is up to you to use hidden aspects as selling points.

Energy Use. Energy use is a partially hidden aspect of every house. A buyer can't actually see it, but he or she will want to investigate the system. Homeowners and buyers are both more conscious of, and knowledgeable about, energy efficiency. The first time a client looks at your house, he or she will probably ask about its energy-saving features. Be prepared to give realistic answers.

What are the heat and utility bills in January and February? Air conditioning in summer? Have your utility statements at hand to back up your information. A knowledgeable buyer will pay particular attention to the way the house sits on the lot. A house with most of its windows to the south and a long roof overhang picks up warmth from a low-lying winter sun that can shine in below the overhang. The same arrangement protects the house in summer when the sun is high. The overhang shades it and prevents sunlight from beating in through the window and overheating it. Trees can also provide shade in summer and insulation against harsh winds in winter. If a prospect doesn't notice these energy-savers, point them out and explain their benefits.

Maintenance. Another hidden factor can be maintenance. Some houses are more difficult to keep up than others. And some people are more interested than others in cleaning and working around the house. What are the maintenance aspects of your house? Be prepared to answer questions about maintenance fully.

For example, wood floors are more difficult to maintain than carpeting or linoleum and tile but, if properly cared for, they are extremely beautiful and a valuable selling point. If you have a special simple way of caring for your wood floors, explain it.

Be prepared to describe everything about upkeep of all the surfaces (inside cupboards and closets, too), appliances, hardware, heating and cooling equipment, and plumbing. Newer houses tend to be built with maintenance care in mind. Floors, inside and outside walls, landscaping, and so on, are planned with the modern family in mind—where household help is minimal and both husband and wife often work outside the home.

Older houses are less likely to have as many maintenance-free aspects. But any older house that has been well cared for will have a system of its own when it comes to maintenance. As the seller, you should tell the buyer everything you can about how you keep the house in shape. This will be a major consideration for a buyer, especially if the house is old, because it will become his or her obligation as a homeowner to maintain the house properly. In some mortgage loans, the lender stipulates that the borrower must maintain the house and property to a certain standard, so help the buyer in this respect.

All of these considerations will increase the price of your house. And there is one more major hidden aspect that lends your house prestige—and, incidentally, adds dollars to the price tag.

Future Value

How much you can ask for your house now is largely based on what we real estate brokers call its future value. The potential value of a house is an important selling point. Whether or not it appreciates relates directly to community and performance: how a house functions—maintenance, repair, energy, and so on.

Every buyer—even a family that plans to live in a house for a lifetime—always considers its resale value. Most Americans live in a house for only two to three years before they move to a new location or "trade up." The ability to sell a house easily for its proper price depends on more than current demand and financing. It depends a great deal on the nature of the house.

Some houses will have better resale value than others. A three-bedroom, two-bath home, for example, will sell more easily than a two-bedroom one.

Even if the buyer plans never to resell the house, he or she will want the equity and appreciation of the property to grow. Any repairs, remodeling, additions of a bath or family room, can make a profound difference in the overall value. (See Chapter 5 for long-term improvements that will increase the value of a house.)

For example, improving ceiling and wall insulation can greatly upgrade energy efficiency, increasing the future value of the house and at the same time immediately saving money in fuel costs.

Location and Neighborhood. Expensive remodeling won't affect the value of a house if the property is in the wrong place.

In general, an old house, even in poor condition, in a good neighborhood has better future value than a good house in a declining one. A house in one neighborhood may increase in value while its close counterpart in another neighborhood can drop in value because of deterioration in the area. And a new house may rapidly lose value if the neighborhood starts to go downhill. The value of an older house may increase as the neighborhood becomes more desirable.

If the property is right—good neighborhood or growing community—the value will endure and grow in the future. Often, deteriorating neighborhoods are slated for renovation, and development and property in them can be a good investment over the long term.

There are many things about a neighborhood that a prospective buyer can see or discover without their being pointed out. But, as the seller, you should be thoroughly familiar with the future plans of the community in order to use them as selling points.

The evaluation of a property always rests with the buyer. But when you carefully assess your own property you can push the sale along. Answer questions fully and shape your main selling points to reduce confusion and help the buyer see your house clearly and in a good light.

Property evaluation is a process that often requires a great deal of experience and knowledge by persons in the real estate business. But if you follow the steps outlined here, it is a process whose principles are easy to comprehend.

4

What a Buyer Will Look For

Two out of every three homeowners buy a used house. The biggest advantage an older house offers is more space for the money. Landscaping has often been taken care of. In older, well-established neighborhoods, taxes are usually stable; schools, offices, and other essential destinations are nearby or within a reasonable distance.

But many older houses are located in decaying neighborhoods, although many such areas are undergoing improvement today. If this is your situation, check on any future plans for neighborhood improvement, urban renewal, or land appropriation for new highways and other projects. I have found that future development can be a major selling point in an up-and-coming area.

Buyer Inspection

A knowledgeable buyer will want to make a thorough inspection of your house to look for hidden defects and obvious remodeling needs. It's not unusual for a buyer to obtain an expert appraisal of the property to establish its value and point out deficiencies. In many cities there are reputable inspection

27

firms that will examine the house for a moderate fee and give a detailed report on the wiring, plumbing, septic tank, and heating plant.

How Old Is Old?

The age of your house is not necessarily a limitation. While older homes may require more repair work, if you have given your house excellent care, it will compare favorably with newer structures. Show prospective buyers all upkeep records, including service calls and new installations.

If a buyer calls in experts, suggest that he or she first check their reputation and references; some unscrupulous operators justify their fee by exaggerating flaws which they seek to repair at inflated costs.

If it appears that repairs and improvements are needed, the buyer should secure estimates of the cost of the work, and these repairs can be a negotiating point of the sale.

As the seller, you can anticipate in advance what the buyer will be looking for in a house inspection. There are nine areas that usually demand special attention:

1. *Termite infestation and wood rot.* A check by a termite specialist is essential, particularly in those areas of the country that have a history of infestation. A wise buyer will want a termite clause inserted in the sales contract, giving certification of inspection and guarantee (but it is generally up to the buyer to get this inspection).

For more information about how to detect signs of pest infestation, see Chapter 5, "Putting Your House in Order."

2. *Structural failure.* The buyer will examine the construction for a sagging roof, cracked walls or slabs, uneven floors, and other evidence of supporting soil which has poor bearing capacity or inadequate structural fastenings.

Opened joints, buckled wallboards, or cracks in the plaster can indicate serious problems. In a new house, these indicate that poor-quality material was used in construction. In an older house, these signs indicate that the house is shifting on its foundation.

Stains on the walls or ceilings indicate water leaks. Floors should be level and fit closely against the baseboards. If you put wallpaper over cracked, crumbling walls, the buyer is likely to question the condition of the plastering. The quality of tiling or linoleum will also come under inspection. Quality tile and flooring, even if it is old, is always a better selling point than new cheap material put down in haste as a cover-up.

3. *Wiring.* Buyers will check for sufficient amperage and electrical outlets. Is the electrical system throughout your house modern and does it conform to the building code? The buyer is likely to request inspection by the local government for code compliance to make sure the wiring is not dilapidated, exposed, or dangerous. Are there enough outlets and are they located where they are most needed for appliances?

4. *Heating plant.* The general condition of the heating system will be inspected. Is it adequate for the house? Is the system designed so the buyer can add on to the house if he or she wants to? Can a humidifier or air conditioning unit be adapted to it? What is the cost of heating—and cooling—the house? Be prepared to show monthly statements of these costs at different times of the year.

5. *Insulation.* A prospective buyer may ask if the attic and space between interior and exterior walls has been filled with an insulating material. This is a plus selling point. Describe what material was used and how it was installed.

6. *Plumbing.* A home connected to a public sewer system is generally more desirable, in terms of plumbing, than one that relies on a septic tank or a cesspool. Are the water pressure and

drainage system adequate? Is the plumbing modern and does it conform to the building code? Will the buyer be able to add a bathroom if he chooses?

7. *Hot-water heater.* The type and capacity of the tank will be checked to determine if there will be sufficient hot water for family needs. A buyer may ask if your guarantee is still in effect.

8. *Roof and gutters.* A buyer will want to check inside the attic for water stains and discolorations. He or she may ask what kind of roofing material was used and how old it is, or if you have a guarantee for the roof.

9. *Basements.* You cannot hide a damp basement. Is yours structurally sound? Signs of water penetration will show around the foundation walls. A sump pump in the basement is a sure tipoff that the basement leaks.

Any faults in the above list can reduce the price of your house. It's to your advantage to check them yourself and make repairs before you show the house (unless you are willing to drop the price to make up for defects).

Also examine the condition of the outside paint, and the paint and wallpaper inside. All windows and doors should work properly and be in good repair. If there is a fireplace, it should have a workable damper. Carefully check the floor and wall tile, and fixtures in the bathroom; if the tile needs recaulking, do a good job. An immaculate bathroom is a plus selling point.

Most buyers realize there is no such thing as a perfect house. But the better condition it is in, the more likely you are to get your price.

A New House

If you are selling a new house, buyers will look for a somewhat different set of standards. As the seller, to avoid misunderstanding and unnecessary complications at the closing, you can help yourself, and the buyer, by being specific:

Describe exactly which features are provided with the new house. Any extra features that are to be included in the finished house should be put in writing. Complications arise if a buyer assumes an item is included and later discovers he or she has misunderstood.

Describe exactly all costs that you, as the builder and seller, will assume. (These might include street paving, water and sewer lines, and so on.)

A prospective buyer will want to know the zoning laws. The neighborhood may be strictly residential or zoned for certain commercial uses. This information could affect future property values.

If you are building a house to sell, it's not unusual for a buyer to check construction progress regularly while the house is being built.

The day before closing, I have never known a buyer who didn't want to make a final, thorough inspection trip. This is the last chance to check all equipment, windows and doors, and request changes.

A buyer will want the following papers when taking possession of a new house:

1. Warranties from all manufacturers for equipment in the house;
2. Certificate of occupancy;
3. Certificates from the Health Department clearing plumbing and sewer installations;
4. All applicable certificates of code compliance.

31

An Information Sheet

Keeping a seller's information sheet can help you group together your selling points. It is the sort of thing that the best real estate brokers do to keep track of the important elements in the sale.

SELLER'S INFORMATION SHEET

Type of house_____ Age_____

Number of floors_____

Exterior surface_____

Exterior paint_____

Roof condition_____ Gutters_____

Interior walls, type & cond._____

Floors, type & cond._____

Basement condition_____

Attic_____

Wiring & elec. serv._____

Water pipes/plumbing_____

Septic/sewer_____

Water supply_____

Hot water_____

Heating cost, per year_____

Heating system_____

Insulation_____

Storm windows & screens_____

Kitchen & laundry equip._____

Fireplaces_____

Doors & windows_____

Tiling, cond._____

Landscaping_____

Assessor's map_____ Lot size_____

Easements_____ Outbuildings_____

Assessment_____ Taxes_____

Price, asking_____ Mortgages_____

Time limits_____

General remarks:_____

_____

_____

_____

5

Putting Your House in Order

There is a mournful look about a house that is no longer loved. The grass is shaggy, dirty windows look dolefully onto the street, paint peels as from a nervous rash, and, when you step inside, the whole structure seems to heave a sigh.

When you want to sell your house, you may no longer feel any love for it, but if you want your house to sell, somebody will have to love it. And it is difficult to love a house with a shabby, neglected air.

Once you have decided to sell, your first thought should be to put your house in shape for sale. It may be necessary to re-decorate, to paint, wallpaper, and fix all those little things you've neglected so long that you don't notice them anymore.

But a prospective buyer will notice—and will immediately spot signs of neglect. I was about to close a sale once, at very advantageous terms for the seller, when the buyer tried to open a door and the knob came off in his hand. That little incident made an easy sale difficult and cost the seller a couple of thousand dollars.

When you begin to get your house ready to be sold, you should decide just how much money and effort you are willing to expend. Often, a few hundred dollars spent will realize thousands when you sell. But your money should be spent wisely.

Long-Term Improvements and Additions

When the time has come to sell, you will no longer be in the market for major renovations or additions, but those that have been made may have increased the value of your house considerably. Behind many home improvements is the idea that you are increasing the future value of your investment. At one time, real estate people thought that individuality in improvements did not increase the value of a home much. "People don't want to pay for out-of-the-ordinary extras," was the thinking.

That has changed, and the extra stamp of individuality on a house can bring big dividends. An unusual deck, a small plant room with a skylight, and extra features in the kitchen or bathroom will greatly enhance the value of a house. One realtor said about a house she knew, "The former owners put $45,000 into a kitchen-family room with skylights and they got an extra $100,000 for the house."

According to many people in the business, renovation of bathrooms and kitchens is an excellent investment. Enlarged bathrooms with large windows and up-to-date accoutrements such as a whirlpool bath and a bidet make a house more attractive to a prospective buyer. But the kitchen is probably the most important room in the house at selling time.

Custom features such as butcher block counters, built-ins, extra storage space, and a work island make a house highly desirable.

Any custom work should be of the best-quality materials. One of my associates, a Connecticut broker, says, "Home buyers really dislike anything 'plasticized' like acoustical tiles, fake beams, and phony paneling."

In addition to his or her personal requirements, there are certain inherent virtues that every buyer looks for in a house. Proportion and good exterior lines head the list. Windows and doors that are balanced and correctly placed make the best impression. The exterior materials should be consistent and match the style of the house (mixes of wood, stone, stucco, and brick give a house a haphazard appearance). Whether a house is contemporary, traditional, colonial, or modern, it should have style and consistent design. This doesn't mean that every house needs to be an architect's masterpiece, but neither should it be a jumble of ideas and afterthoughts.

So whenever you think about making additions or improvements to your property, bear in mind the overall effect.

While the cost of the extras you have already put into your house can very often be retrieved, and even earn a profit, high-priced additions can reach a point of diminishing returns. A swimming pool, for example, can add too much to the price of a home, making it a much more difficult sale, particularly in areas of the country where its use is limited. An investment in a pool or a greenhouse isn't made with only a possible return in mind, but for the pleasure these things provide over a period of years.

Energy Efficiency

Features that today can pay off handsomely when you sell are energy-savers. Extra insulation, storm windows, weatherstripping, and other ways of reducing energy use are highly prized, and buyers are more sophisticated than ever before about them. They ask about the R-factor of insulation, the wiring, the plumbing, the septic system, and in general want to be sure that a house is in good and efficient working order in addition to the more aesthetic considerations.

If you can show a prospective buyer a house that is more energy efficient, you greatly increase your chances of getting your price in today's market.

Passive and active solar systems, windmills, and similar features can be expensive, although they often carry tax benefits along with them. But with little or no expenditures, you can make your house more energy efficient by following some specific recommendations:

Air Conditioning

Maintain the efficiency of your air conditioning system by changing or cleaning the air filters every month or two. A service professional should check the cooling surfaces at least every two years. Once a year, bearings should be lubricated and the fan belt—which transmits power from motor to blower—checked for tension and adjusted. At proper tension, the belt can be pressed down between ¼ and ½ inch, at a point midway between the motor and blower when the power is shut off.

Be sure the outside condenser is kept clean and is located where air flow will be unimpeded by shrubbery or nearby walls.

Insulate air conditioning ducts where they pass through attics or other uncooled areas, using at least two inches of insulating material. Carefully seal the area around a window air conditioner.

In warm weather, operate exhaust fans periodically when cooking, bathing, or doing laundry. Use covered cooking dishes, particularly when boiling.

Turn on window units only when needed and turn them off when the rooms they cool are unoccupied. When a central air conditioning system is operating, close doors to unused rooms. Generally, it's best to leave the registers open to keep the entire system in balance.

Start your air conditioner early in the day or run it on the thermostat. During periods of peak demand for power, move the thermostat to a higher setting. This reduces the load on the system during critical demand periods to help reduce the risk of brownouts. The system uses the most power when starting and running through the initial cooling period. A higher thermostat setting will keep the compressor from constant starting and turning off.

Keep doors and windows shut and keep storm windows in place during the air conditioning season. Close fireplace vents.

Plant trees, install heat-absorbing or reflecting glass panes, awnings, or overhangs at windows exposed to the sun. Use light-colored materials on exterior surfaces of the house. This reduces solar heat absorption from window glass and lowers the need for operating cooling fans or air conditioners.

If attic crawl space is inaccessible for insulating, install an attic fan controlled by a thermostat set for 110 degrees or another predetermined high. This draws off accumulated warm air under the roof and reduces summer need for air conditioning or constant attic fan operation.

Appliances

Make sure refrigerator and freezer door seals are airtight and that condensing coils are clean.

Defer heavy use of the cooking range and self-cleaning features of the oven to periods when the air conditioner's load is lightest—late in the evening and early in the morning. Schedule use of washer, dryer, or iron for low-demand periods.

Heating

Insulate your home. There should be at least six inches of insulation over the top floor ceiling and at least three or four in exterior walls. Check with an expert before insulating exterior walls; improper insulation may cause moisture condensation.

Install weatherstripping at windows and door joints, caulk door and window frames, and seal cracks in exterior walls. This will prevent air leaks that permit heat to escape in cold weather and infiltrating warm air to tax the air conditioning system or unit in hot weather.

Install storm windows or insulating glass. Close window drapes at night.

Check the efficiency of your heating plant to be sure heat exchange surfaces and air filters are clean and that air combustion is correctly adjusted. A professional should make necessary adjustments.

Seal any indoor air leaks between living areas and the attic—floor cracks and loose attic doors. Keep attic well vented to the outdoors.

Pest Infestation

Today's more sophisticated home buyer will also want to be sure that there are no serious problems with destructive pests. To be able to give your house a clean bill of health, you should know something about wood-destroying insects and fungi which can cause damage to a house. Early detection of pests and decay can help you avoid expensive repairs.

Damp-wood termites are found in southern Florida, the Southwestern states, and along the Pacific Coast. Preferring damp wood, they rarely damage houses but may be found in house construction where wet lumber is used.

Dry-wood termites are found in a narrow strip along the Atlantic Coast from Cape Henry, Virginia, to the Florida Keys, westward along the coast of the Gulf of Mexico to the Pacific Coast, and into northern California. There also is a local infestation in Tacoma, Washington. Dry-wood termites are a serious problem in parts of the tropics, including Puerto Rico and Hawaii.

You can spot damage by clean cavities cut across the grain in solid dry wood. The cavities may contain slightly compressed pellets of partially digested wood resembling coarse sand or sawdust. Piles of pellets accumulate under the push-out holes through which the termites clear their work areas.

Subterranean termites are the most destructive of all wood-destroying insects in the United States. They heavily infest California, the Mississippi and Ohio River valleys, and the Southern United States roughly around South Carolina, Georgia, Alabama, Mississippi, Louisiana, Florida, and eastern Texas. Other parts of the United States experience moderate to slight infestation. Hawaii and Puerto Rico are heavily infested; Alaska has no termite activity.

Damage may not be noticeable on wood surfaces because termites burrow inside the material they attack. You can see tunnels along the grain of the wood and specks of excrement when the exterior surface of a timber is stripped away. Often the wood is completely honeycombed, leaving only a thin shell.

When the subterranean termites cannot gain direct access to wood from the soil, they build tubes of earth and partly digested wood, crossing such obstacles as concrete or brick foundation walls, and even the "termite shields" provided by some builders.

Carpenter ants often attack the columns on open porches and wooden windowsills. Their presence is indicated by hol-

41

low, irregular, clean chambers cut across the grain of partially decayed wood and by piles of fine-to-coarse wood fibers removed from the chambers they construct as nesting places. Sound wood near the nest also may be damaged.

Flatheaded borers complete a life cycle in one or two years but may live for thirty or forty years before emerging from infested wood. Larvae three or four years old are found in the woodwork of buildings standing for only one or two years, showing that stored lumber is a source of infestation. Borers leave an elliptical, tunneled imperfection in wood. They do not reinfest seasoned lumber, so treatment is usually unnecessary when signs of infestation are found in existing construction.

Powder-post beetles infest hardwood flooring, leaving an accumulation of fine dust and powder around a hole in the wood. A spray insecticide will control them in most cases, although fumigation by a pest-control company may be necessary.

Decay

Wood decay is caused by airborne spores which produce minute, plantlike growths called fungi, consisting of numerous microscopic threads. Fungi work in damp wood to cause decay. In the final stages of decay, however, the wood is often dry.

White decay fungi is usually caused by improper ventilation, or by inadequate flashing, vapor barriers, or surface sealant.

Brown decay causes wood fibers to shrink, crack, and crumble. Decay is evident behind painted surfaces when a light tap on the suspected area with the handle of a screwdriver or knife produces a dead sound. Usually the painted surface will be severely checked at the decay area.

Damage Check

For a complete inspection and eradication of pests, one should call a reputable pest-control company. Check areas where termites gain access, such as grade-level entrances, garages, exterior stairs, an inadequate protective slope around the house, or places where siding extends close to the ground. Examine exterior walls and crawl spaces for termite tubes, using a small hammer to sound walls, windowsills and frames for damage. A dead sound indicates decay; a hollow sound indicates possible termite infestation.

With a sharp instrument such as a knife or ice pick, probe exposed wood posts, landings, stairways, entrance door frames and thresholds, garage sills and studs, and any areas where wooden structural elements come near the ground. Move stacked lumber or firewood that is stored against or near the building.

In the basement, where pests are attracted by furnace warmth, check the intersection of floor slab with chimney and foundation, areas where pipes penetrate the foundation, and stair carriages where joints contact foundation wall or floor slab. If the house is built with foundation slabs on a grade, or with part of the basement finished, termites may enter undetected behind furred walls.

Any inspector will look for piles of wood dust sifted down beside baseboards, or for bulging or loose wallboard finish. Examine the area under heating elements for wood dust or partly digested wood, and check partition sills by flashlight for signs of pest infestation or decay.

Because termites need moisture to live, an inspector would check bathroom partitions and flooring around toilets where water leaks and condensation may cause decay and attract

43

pests. Pay careful attention to girders and other critical structural members which, if damaged, may weaken the structure of the house. Check floor joists, sills, or beams bearing on the foundation.

Treatment

Termite activity in buildings can be controlled by chemical treatment of the soil. This is a practical and economical method for preventing infestation before construction of new houses, and for controlling it in older ones. Soil treatment chemicals generally used are aldrin, dieldrin, heptachlor or chlordane. All of these are chlorinated hydrocarbons.

The people in my industry have to be knowledgeable about termites, fungi, and other infestations. If you want to sell your own house, you too should be familiar with their signs.

Landscaping

While extensive relandscaping should not be necessary to sell your house, the property should look neat and cared for. Hedges and bushes should be trimmed and the grass cut. While home buyers like nice landscaping touches, they often shy away from property that requires a good deal of maintenance. Sweeping lawns that must be mowed frequently, and flower-beds that need constant attention, do not attract most buyers today.

Rather, attractive and maintenance-free ground cover such as myrtle and pachysandra are attractive to those who seek natural beauty without bother.

When you are readying your house for sale, extensive landscaping is ordinarily not worth the money and effort. But the grass should be mowed, hedges and bushes trimmed, dead leaves raked, and any trees or plants should be healthy—if there is a dead limb on a tree, have it cut away.

Short-Term Checklist

Look all around the house, from top to bottom. You can be sure that a prospective buyer will examine everything. There may be small problems that you won't notice—you've gotten used to the switch that's upside-down, the leaking faucet, and the broken light fixtures. It may be a good idea to have someone else come into your house and look for things that need to be fixed. You could hire a handyman or ask a friend, or have someone from the hardware store come over.

While major renovation is not necessary, a coat of paint over dingy walls, or new wallpaper, will do a great deal toward making your house more attractive. But stick to neutral colors and patterns. Don't do a slapdash job and be sure to use quality paints and other materials.

Clean all the closets. Rearrange closets and spread the clothing around rather than having some closets crammed full and others almost empty. Orderly closets and cupboards look bigger, and also impress the buyer that your house, if he or she buys it, will be in good condition when it is time to move in.

Rearrange the bedrooms so there is no extra furniture in any of them to give a closed-in feeling to the room. Use bright, fresh-looking bedspreads and curtains.

Kitchens take top priority these days—light and a feeling of spaciousness are the requirements. If your kitchen is small and dark, compensate by keeping it sparkling clean. Scrub the countertops—put away all small appliances. All dishes, canned goods, cleaning supplies, and so on should be tidily tucked away. Make sure your stove, oven, and refrigerator are immaculate.

The idea behind clean, neat closets, cupboards, and appliances is not to prove that you're a good housekeeper, or even that the house will be in move-in condition. The real idea that gets across subliminally is that a seller who keeps the showable portion of the house in good condition also maintains its other "hidden" aspects—heating, plumbing, wiring, and the rest. (Incidentally, this is usually true.)

Now, make up your checklist:

Home Seller's Checklist

1. Are the hedges trimmed, the grass cut, the driveway clear?
2. If there is a pool, does it work? (Many of them don't.)
3. Has the septic system been cleaned lately? When?
4. Patio and decks painted and clean?
5. Roof and gutters OK? Any leaks?
6. Is the garage clean? Can you park two cars in the two-car garage?
7. Is the basement clean? If it is used for storage, is everything stacked and stored neatly?
8. Do the washer and dryer work?
9. Is there a water problem? Has it been corrected? (People come to look at houses in rainy weather, too.)
10. Is the electrical system in good condition?
11. Is the furnace in good working order? Is it serviced periodically? Is the hot water heater owned or is it rented? (You can't sell what you don't own.)
12. Is the exterior paint OK?
13. In the interior—are there cracks or water marks on the ceilings?
14. Is the paint or woodwork, or the flooring, badly scratched, cracked or broken?
15. Are the fireplaces in working order?

16. Do all the doors and windows fit?
17. Are the storm windows on or available?
18. Are all the fixtures in working order?
19. Are all the kitchen appliances in working order?
20. Are all the closets neat, clean, and in order?

Make Sure That You Have:

1. Listing sheets giving pertinent details to include cost of oil, water, gas, taxes, assessments, electricity, and so on.
2. A listing of what does and does not go with the house.
3. Items that are negotiable.
4. A date when you can show the house.
5. A target date for vacating the house after it is sold.
6. An asking price $_____. A price you will accept $_____.

6

6 Rms. Rv. Vu

Your house is in great shape. The hedges are trimmed, trees pruned, lawn mowed. The windows are all sparkling. You think, "Do I really want to sell it?" And then decide that you do. But how to find the buyers?

First, tell everyone you know that your house is for sale and the price you are asking. Tell not only all of your friends, but the local merchants and your postman. Tell as many people as you can without becoming an absolute bore. You can let a sizable number of persons who just might be in the market know about the availability of your house.

This word-of-mouth advertising is free, and it often gets results. Also, since it doesn't cost anything, you have more negotiating room, although some people who immediately find a hot prospect will not negotiate because it all seemed too easy.

Type a sales notice with a description of your house twice on each half of an 8½ x 11-inch sheet of paper. Have a number of copies made, cut the sheets in half, and put them up on bulletin boards at supermarkets, organizations such as church groups and the "Y," and anywhere it is allowed. At the same time, you might want to put a FOR SALE sign on your lawn, depending on local regulations and whether your neighbors object, and also whether you want to see prospective buyers at any time.

Throughout the United States, many towns have ordinances against FOR SALE signs, routinely passed by community legislative bodies in the past. The American Civil Liberties Union is currently challenging these regulations. One long-time resident of a New York community, however, spent a day in jail because he refused to remove a two-foot, 20-inch sign in his window which said HOUSE FOR SALE—BY APPOINTMENT ONLY.

If you haven't sold your house with word-of-mouth, bulletin board, and FOR SALE sign advertising, it is time to prepare an advertisement for the newspaper.

Realtors as a rule of thumb say that an advertising budget for the sale of a house should be as much as one percent of the sales price. Unless the price of your house is well into the middle or high six figures, the best place for real estate ads is in the real estate listings of local newspapers. Of course, if you have a beautiful and very expensive home, the best ad is a picture of it, a full explanation of the marvels to be found inside, and a glowing description of the grounds. This display ad, placed in magazines or newspapers or even on local television, is the best sales vehicle. But it is expensive.

For most people, the classifieds—the marketplace for all of the houses in the area—are the answer. The weekend listings are generally read by most men and women who are seriously in the market.

Of course, every other house for sale is also listed, so the competition demands that you catch the buyer's eye and get him or her interested enough to read your ad.

You will probably find hundreds of house ads in the paper at one time. Even though they may be broken down geographically, one ad often looks like all the rest.

The headline is the eye-catcher. If the headline captures his or her interest, the reader will continue. But don't try to be cute. Pick one outstanding feature and tell about it. If your house overlooks a golf course, a river, mountains, farmlands, and has a panoramic view, that should be in the headline. If there is history in your house, talk about it. If the grounds are beautifully landscaped and look like an estate or park, say that. If your home is spacious and perfect for entertaining, use it.

If there are lots of children in your neighborhood and the streets are safe to play in, say so. If you're near a beach, have an ocean view, or can walk to the ocean, mention it.

Lead off with what is positive and out of the ordinary.

Your ad should have a unique approach to the sale rather than a mere recitation of the house's features. It should speak directly and personally to the reader. Be concise—cut out all unnecessary words, but never delete a useful sales word just because it reduces the cost a little.

Be precise—don't say "near shopping" when you could say "five-minute walk to shopping." Use common, everyday language. Do not use tired old catchphrases such as "best buy in town." Give as much information as you can. Don't exaggerate—if your house can't possibly live up to the expectation created, you have no chance of making a sale.

Mention that you are selling the house yourself by using the phrase "by owner" in the ad.

Some realtors think that you should not state the price of the house, that it will put off persons who are only looking. I think that you should always give the price. It's the first thing any prospective buyer wants to know, and even many "lookers" will skip by ads with no price. You don't have to give the exact price, however—a price range is satisfactory. But you are wasting a prospect's time—and your own time—if you don't give at least a ballpark figure.

The following sample classifieds were given to me by a national real estate firm. They are ads that have been found in the business to be most successful in attracting buyers. Read them carefully and try to use the ideas found in them in writing an ad for your own home.

Don't write just one ad—write several. After you have composed them, leave them and do something else for a while. When you come back, read them again and then pick the one you think does the best selling job.

ON A SCALE OF I TO I0

This newly listed executive 2-story has got to be a 10. The 2200 sq. ft. of finished living area incls. 4 bdrms. (Large master bdrm. with dressing area and full bath). Formal dining-rm., breakfast rm., family rm., with fireplace, 3 baths, double oven, 2-car att. garage and nicely land-scaped and fenced yard. Priced at $46,900. Be the first to see this

"U"
"O"
"YOURSELF"

The opportunity to purchase this especially constructed home of a commercial builder. A special site was selected on 2 wooded and rustic estate lots in an area of beautiful homes. This rambling pink stone features 4 bedrooms, den, 2½ baths, or 3 bedrooms, and a basement recreation room. No cost has been spared to make this a showplace of East Dallas. Must be seen to be appreciated. Priced below reproduction at $57,500. CALL for an appointment today!

It's Beautiful

The picture just couldn't do justice to our new four bedroom two story English Manor House finished in mossy native stone and nestled among the trees on a corner lot. You enter through double doors into the sumptious foyer with its classic turned stairway. The formal living room is on your left and an elegant bay windowed dining room is on your right. A country kitchen and breakfast room look out over a cov-ered patio deck with a mile of scenic

Rembrandt Couldn't Paint

A prettier picture than this cool, snowwhite rambler framed in setting of towering shade trees. Wide greeting hall entry to HOMEY den (with Dutch tile fireplace) with screened porch views of patio and gardens. Away-from-it-all RUMPUS ROOM with coke bar, fireplace! Three larger-than-ordinary oedrooms plus master garden view and dressing room! Greenhouse and More! Take time to SEE TODAY! Your offer

Every Day Is Lady's Day

This attractive 1½ story brick, 1858 S. RAINBOW DR. (Corner McLean) is not just the average home — it is SOMETHING EXTRA with 3 bdrm or 2 & den, 2½ baths, studio, breezeway — glassed in, lovely brick wall enclosed patio & barbe-cue. Central air & heat. Carpeting, lighted closets, mirrors. COME SEE FOR YOURSELF!

SO NOW THERE'S JUST THE TWO OF YOU

Just large enough, but not too large for you. 2 bedrooms, one for the grandchildren, den or fam-ily room, formal dining room with mirrored wall, large storage area, all built-in kitchen includ-ing desk and china closet, new refrigeration unit, block fence, just recently redecorated, new custom draperies, w/w carpet-ing, large covered patio with in-door/outdoor carpeting. Arcadia

REMEMBER WHEN

rooms were spacious & quality was real? When there were basements & attics? & fireplaces? When you walked to school, parks, shops, & bus? Few of us remember when Rockefeller first invested in Real Estate, but he did! Might he have begun with something like this N.W. Duplex? Why not start mak-ing your rich memories for $29,900?

7

Showing the House

Many people decide to use a realtor to sell their house just because they would rather not do the job themselves. I have shown many houses that could as easily have been shown by the owner. It is much easier to be away—to have someone else take prospective buyers through the house. But if you really want to sell it yourself, you must put up with upset schedules and a certain loss of privacy. You must also learn how to perform some of the realtor's functions yourself, such as selling when you seem to be chatting, and closing a sale.

Before the prospective buyer arrives, check the house one last time and make sure it's ready for viewing.

Polishing Up and Setting the Scene

Make sure the front door is clean and looks inviting—it is the first thing the buyer will notice.

Open draperies, blinds, and curtains so that there is plenty of light and the house looks cheerful.

Remove all those little *objets d'art* and bric-a-brac on tables and in corners. The cluttered look often conveys a cramped feeling.

Keep the stairways clear.

Make sure that bathrooms are sparkling clean. Replace shower curtains if necessary. Tubs and showers should be properly caulked and free of mildew. Throw away old bottles in the medicine cabinet and arrange the cabinet neatly.

Replace burned-out bulbs in lamps, fixtures, hallways, closets, cellar, and so on.

If you have pets, your house may have odors you don't notice anymore. Check this carefully—ask your friends if they notice pet odors. If so, find the source of the trouble and correct it. If you don't, you can lose a sale the moment an interested person steps across the threshold. Your house should smell as fresh and clean as it looks.

Keep your pets out of the way; if necessary, send them over to a neighbor's house.

Meeting the Prospect

Don't try to force conversation—this is a business, not a social occasion. Try to be relaxed and easy. You will show the house by appointment only, but you can't become upset just because a prospective buyer is late (they usually are), or doesn't show up, or hangs around until your dinner is cold and the children are crying. Everyone in the household must understand that during this time, selling the home takes first priority. After you have dealt with the first visitor, you will be an old pro.

Be prepared with all documents that substantiate the cost of running the house: the amount of fuel that you use, electric bills, tax statements, and water bills, for example.

Also have on hand the location of any wells or septic tanks.

Some successful realtors recommend that you always have something in the oven when a prospective buyer arrives. A turkey is good; it makes people remember happy Thanksgivings. But it can be a little expensive to pop a turkey in the oven every time a prospect drops in. "Bake bread," says one realtor. The smell of baking bread is a warm, pleasant aroma that makes people feel at home. Chicken soup, or any homemade soup, will also fill your house with inviting aromas. It could make the buyer's mouth water in more ways than one.

The Show Route

The easiest way to show the house is along regular traffic patterns. Let the buyers look around, then let them follow their own pace. Don't keep up a running line of chatter, but encourage their questions and be sure you have all the answers—where the schools are and how they rate, where the bus stops and how often, how far it is to the shopping center, and what time the mail is delivered.

You can usually tell right away whether potential buyers are interested or not. If there is no interest, make the tour a short one. That will be easy, because they will want to leave quickly if the house is obviously unsuitable. Buyers don't want to waste their time, either. If prospects recognize immediately that the house is wrong for them, they will probably say so. Accept this for what it is—a graceful time-saver. Don't push people to go through the house when they are clearly apathetic.

Don't worry if buyers express interest but want to come back with wives, husbands, mothers-in-law, architects, best friends, or whomever. The average buyer looks at a house four times before deciding, and sales are almost never made on the first visit.

Most prospective homebuyers who take the trouble to call for an appointment and show up are seriously in the market, not just shoppers.

In most cases, they look at ten to twelve houses over a period of three to six months before purchasing. When it's down to a choice between three or four, they are ready to buy.

Sizing Up Prospects

You should size up prospects in five different ways:

First, find out how many houses they have seen and how long they have been looking.

Second, when do they want to move in?

Third, is your house within a comfortable price range, or will a downpayment and financing be a problem?

Fourth, must they sell their own home before purchasing another? Is there a fluidity problem? Can they make a decision and act on it or are there other problems to be solved before making a move?

Fifth, what is the factor that will make them want to buy your house? What is it that is most important—and is that factor present in your house?

The best way to find out all these things is to draw out your clients. Let them talk while you do a little creative listening.

The first question a buyer asks himself or herself is, can I really afford to buy this house? The key question is how much can be spent on the property, based on income and expenses.

Here are two ways buyers estimate their ability to meet house payments. As the seller you should also know these factors.

1. The price of the house should be no more than two-and-one-half times the buyer's annual income. Younger people should limit the payment to twice their annual income, unless they have substantial income or especially promising job prospects.

2. No more than 35 percent of income should be allowed for

monthly housing expenses—including mortgage payment, heat, utilities, repairs, and maintenance.

A buyer needs to estimate carefully how much money can be spent for monthly mortgage and utilities payments and property maintenance. You can help by providing figures on typical monthly payments for the house and also help estimate maintenance costs.

The buyer also must figure the initial, one-time-only expenses of closing the sale. Closing costs are often more than a new homeowner expects. The Real Estate Settlement Procedures Act of 1974 (RESPA) regulates lending practices, and closing and settlement procedures, to eliminate unnecessary costs and difficulties. Read carefully the section on settlement costs in Chapter 12, "The Closing."

It's important that the buyer have a realistic view of all the costs. If he chooses your house and discovers later it's too expensive, he might get in over his head. Once a prospect takes a liking to a house, it can become an obsession, causing the person to twist every which way trying to figure out a way to buy it. Even if he or she manages to put the deal together, it may fall through at the last minute. Or he may have to bail out. If you have helped with financing, you can be hurt. It is to everyone's advantage to realistically appraise a buyer's ability to carry the financial burden of the house.

When showing your house, never argue with a prospective buyer or try to defend your house. Just outline its best features and try to get the person to see what living in the house would be like.

Don't push or oversell—after all, your house must sell itself, and the best way that you can show the house is to step aside and let it shine.

8

New Ways to Sell a House

American ingenuity continues to amaze. With the highest interest rates and the most sluggish real estate market in memory, homeowners who want to sell have been borrowing methods from other marketplaces—from used car lots to Arabian bazaars.

General Motors, holding $10 million worth of houses taken over from transferred employees, has been offering a free automobile with each house sold. The gimmick appeared to be a good tie-in, but GM has found that most of the purchasers prefer a discount off the price of the house to the car.

A couple in Illinois offered an all-expenses-paid trip to Hawaii as an incentive to buy their home. This ploy got them a large number of shoppers, but when it was sold, the buyer preferred to deduct the cost of the trip from the sales price to actually taking hula lessons in Honolulu.

All over the country, owners are offering various incentives to create interest and sales, such as new wardrobes, furniture, and boats.

A family in Wisconsin ran a contest. As the prize, they put up their $79,000 farmhouse and fifty-one acres of farmland. Just write the best ending to: "I want to own a farm in Wisconsin because . . ." in twenty-five words or less. The entry fee was $50. The family reserved the right to cancel the contest and return all the money if they received less than 1,800 entries (equivalent to $90,000). They also said that as many as 3,500 entries would be accepted (making their top price for the farm $175,000).

According to their lawyer, the contest was not a violation of Wisconsin's anti-lottery laws, since winning depends on skill rather than luck. The final word on this contest isn't in yet.

But lotteries and raffles, rather than contests of skill or giveaways, seem to be most popular in the quest to sell houses. In states with anti-lottery laws, homeowners are often getting around the law by taking on as partners charitable organizations, which are often exempt from those laws.

In a Virginia suburb of Washington, D.C., one homeowner anxious to sell teamed up with a local boys' club and sold $100 raffle tickets on his five-bedroom home. He wound up with $113,000, the club received a large contribution, and two teenagers won the house. The boys' club also continued to receive $100 checks long after the lottery had ended.

But things don't always go so smoothly. One California homeowner bought a house on speculation and made expensive improvements that he thought would bring him a substantial profit. But he was unable to sell the house. Eventually he decided to try a lottery and thought he could get around California's anti-lottery laws by taking in the Lighthouse for the Blind as a co-sponsor. But the state refused to accept the scheme, his co-sponsor backed out, and he lost everything in the process.

A woman in Alabama pleaded guilty to a charge of unlawful promotion of gambling after she had tried to raffle off her $60,000 home.

Even in states where raffles are legal, there are potential problems. A couple in Oregon, which allows bingo games although it prohibits lotteries, tried to make their house the prize at a bingo game set up to benefit a local charity, but they couldn't sell enough tickets.

But usually the chance to win a house that sells for $100,000 or more for an investment of $100 or less is enough of an incentive to draw ticket buyers. The major objection seems to be a legal one, although there are no final decisions yet.

New York State's Attorney General, Robert Abrams, has issued an opinion saying that, "The law clearly and explicitly prohibits the conveyance of property by any lottery."

But until the law has been fully tested, many homeowners are willing to take a chance and find that there are charitable organizations willing to risk it with them. The Arthritis Foundation of Syracuse sold $100 tickets on a three-bedroom home in upstate New York, but it has stopped until the legal issues are decided.

Other organizations are going ahead with plans for raffles and lotteries, hoping that their nonprofit status will pacify the authorities.

Even if the charitable organization is allowed to participate in these raffles, the homeowner will not be able to claim a charitable tax deduction, since, according to the Internal Revenue Service, "tax deductions are not given for contributions made in the expectation of a personal return."

9

Negotiating a Deal and Making a Sale

Once you have a buyer who says that he or she wants to buy your house, you can exchange your salesman's hat for your negotiating one. In many cases, I have found that this is what the seller really pays me to do. But it can be done by a knowledgeable seller.

Will he pay your asking price? Usually not. Don't be too anxious to accept the first offer unless you are satisfied, although the first offer is often the best one.

You must first find out whether the person can afford to buy your house. How much cash can he or she put down? The amount will vary, and often depends on how much of the mortgage can be obtained from the bank.

Figuring the Costs

In addition to the downpayment, the buyer will have to pay closing costs, which include, but are not limited to, the lawyer's fee, bank charges, escrow accounts for interest and taxes, filing and registration fees, adjustments for fuel and taxes that you, as the seller, may have paid in advance. Current estimates place closing costs at between 1 and 3 percent of the purchase price.

Selling Price of House	$50,000
Binder 1% (earnest money)	500
	49,500
Contract 10%	
(Binder amount applied)	4,950
Balance due at closing	$44,550
Plus closing costs	

Buyers rarely pay cash. Not many men or women have the lump sum to invest, and tax considerations usually make a cash purchase unwise. Therefore, the buyer usually applies to a bank for a mortgage.

The first thing that the bank wants to know is the dollar amount of the mortgage. Depending on the amount of money the buyer has to put down, mortgages generally range from 70 percent to 90 percent of the purchase price. The bank will consider the buyer's income and the spouse's income, as well as any large outstanding debts.

How Long It Takes

Mortgage approval takes from two to four weeks. In some instances, verbal approval can be secured in a week to ten days. Most buyers will apply to more than one bank or other lending institution.

You must find out the name of the bank where the buyer is applying for the mortgage and then follow up. And remember that until contracts are signed, without any contingencies, you don't have a sale.

Negotiating Points

Assume that your buyer is an eligible one. Arriving at the price he or she is willing to pay and the one you are willing to accept is a matter of negotiation. If the offer is lower than you want, sometimes you can use one or more of the included items as a negotiating point. You might, for example, remove some of the appliances, carpeting, or fixtures. You hope that at some point you will reach a meeting of the minds.

Next, you determine the contingencies. When does the buyer want to take possession?

When can you move out?

How large a mortgage will the buyer need: 75 percent, 80 percent, 85 percent, 90 percent, 95 percent? This is very important for the sale. If the amount the buyer is applying for is a very large percentage of the purchase price, the bank can turn the mortgage down if (1) the price of the property is higher than the appraised value, or (2) the ongoing expense of paying off the mortgage, interest, and maintenance are not warranted by the buyer's income.

For how long does the buyer require the mortgage—twenty, twenty-five, thirty, thirty-five years?

You may be in a position to give the buyer a mortgage yourself. If so, consult your accountant and lawyer first. Read about helping the buyer obtain financing in Chapter 10.

If the buyer needs a building and termite inspection, these should be done within five working days at his or her expense.

You never have a sale until the contracts are signed. Do not stop showing the house. If possible, keep one buyer as a backup. Make sure you tell the second buyer there is a possible buyer and that you will keep them advised. But never sign more than one binder at a time.

Nailing Down the Sale

Until you have a formal contract drawn, as a preliminary step you can prepare an offer to purchase. At the time he or she signs an offer to purchase, it is customary for the buyer to deposit a check in the amount of one percent of the purchase price as earnest money.

The offer to purchase should be filled in completely and signed by all parties. Spell it out. Include anything that is on your mind. This will avoid unnecessary misunderstandings at a later date.

Filling Out the Offer to Purchase

An offer must be for a specified amount in dollars and cents. A full description of the property must be given: land and buildings located at (address) including city or town, and state.

All owners of the property must be listed.

The amount of mortgage the buyer is applying for must be a specified dollars and cents amount. The percentage rate can also be specified or can be shown as "prevailing bank rates."

The number of years must be shown—twenty, twenty-five, thirty years.

Building and termite inspection should be done within five days from the date of offer to purchase.

The closing date can be shown as: "On or before a specified date to be agreed upon between buyer and seller."

Signing of the contracts should be within ten days from the date of the offer to purchase. At this time, the buyer pays the balance of the 10 percent of the purchase price.

Items to be included must be spelled out in detail, such as the refrigerator, stove, or dishwasher.

Items not to be included must also be listed: fixtures, refrigerator, carpeting, and so on.

Items not included can be later negotiated as a separate sale to the buyer.

Attorneys' names and phone numbers should be included, if available.

All copies must be signed. An offer to purchase is worthless unless signed by all parties.

Acceptance by the seller. Whenever possible the binder should be signed by all parties at the time of the agreement. However, the buyer or the seller may want to show the binder to their respective attorneys. In this instance, the number of days for acceptance or rejection must be stipulated.

Any corrections, alterations, or additions to the agreement must be initialed by all parties.

Each party to the agreement must be given a signed copy. A binder check should be held in escrow by the seller's attorney until the contracts are signed and all contingencies are removed.

Keep the House on the Market

The offer to purchase is the first step in a sale. Until the contract is signed, without contingencies, and the buyer gives the seller the specified sum agreed to, there is no firm deal.

In order to avoid losing other potential buyers in the event the deal falls through, the house should not be taken off the market. But all subsequent prospective buyers should be told there is a binder on the property, although final contracts have not been signed.

OFFER TO PURCHASE

I hereby submit an offer of $ _____ for land and buildings located on _____

_____

owned by_____.

Subject to the following conditions:

Obtaining a mortgage loan of $ _____ at _____%, for _____ years within _____ working days.

Satisfactory report of builder's and termite inspection on or before _____

Closing to be on or before _____

Contracts to be signed by buyer on or before _____

Items to be included:_____

_____

_____

Items not to be included:_____

_____

Seller's Attorney_____

Buyer's Attorney _____

This offer to be accepted, or rejected and binder check returned,

within _____ days, subject to a mutually satisfactory contract.

Binder check in the amount of $ _____ attached.

Signed _____ Date _____

Address _____

City & State _____

Accepted by _____

Going to Contract

Once you have accepted the offer, turn everything over to your lawyer for the preparation of the contract. Contracts are generally signed within ten days after the offer to purchase. All contingencies are contained in the contract. At the signing of the contract, the buyer pays the balance agreed upon above the amount of the mortgage.

25% Cash Payment—75% Mortgage	
Selling Price	$50,000
1% Binder	500
(Offer to Purchase)	49,500
9% additional at signing of contract	4,950
	44,550
Mortgage amount loaned by bank	37,500
Amount required above face amount of mortgage (25% – $12,500)	$ 7,050

CONTRACT FOR SALE

....(herein called the "SELLER") of

.... and ....

(herein called the "PURCHASER") of...
hereby make this agreement:

The Seller will sell and convey and the Purchaser will buy that certain piece or parcel of land

situated in the..of..

County of......................................State of...together with

the buildings thereon standing, known as...

......................................and being further described as follows :

TERMS OF PAYMENT :

The full purchase price to be...

.... Dollars.

A deposit of.. Dollars
(the receipt of which is hereby acknowledged by the Seller) is payable upon the execution and delivery of this contract:

ADJUSTMENTS:

Taxes, insurance premiums, water charges, rents, and mortgage interest are to be adjusted as of the date of closing. ....

The premises are conveyed subject to zoning ordinances, building restrictions, and building lines of the...and such restrictions as of record may appear.

CONVEYANCE:

Upon payment in full of the balance due on account of the purchase price with adjustments as provided herein, the Seller will execute and deliver to or upon the order of the Purchaser a Warranty Deed containing full covenants and in the usual form according to Connecticut practice conveying to the Purchaser a good marketable title in and to the above-described premises free and clear of all encumbrances and exceptions of title other than those hereinabove stated to be allowed.

The Deed shall be prepared by the Seller at his expense and shall contain U. S. Documentary stamps on same in the amount required by law at the expense of the Seller.

CLOSING:

The Closing for the delivery of the Deed and the payment of the balance due on account of the purchase price with adjustments shall take place on or before..

RISK OF LOSS:

The risk of loss or damage by fire to the premises as now existing prior to the delivery of the Deed is assumed by the Seller.

BROKERAGE

is recognized as the Broker making the sale, whose Commission is to be paid by the Seller.

SUCCESSION:

This agreement shall inure to the benefit of and shall be binding upon the heirs, legal representatives and assigns of the Seller and Purchaser.

IN WITNESS WHEREOF, the Seller and the Purchaser have executed this agreement, in duplicate, on..........

WITNESSES :

....

....(L.S.)
Seller

....

....(L.S.)
Purchaser

10

Helping the Buyer Buy
Your House

If, like many people now interested in selling their house, you bought a house with a 10 percent downpayment and a thirty-year, 7½-percent mortgage, you were living in a very different world than now exists. Financing a home with mortgages of 19 percent leaves most people searching more for financing than for a place to live. Most Americans cannot qualify for the sort of financing that allowed their parents to purchase houses. Long-term, fixed-interest mortgages are sometimes available these days, but only at the going interest rates of 17 to 19 percent, and with today's average mortgage of $50,000, less than 10 percent of first-time home buyers can qualify.

In the past, a buyer saw your house, it was just right for him and his family and the way they wanted to live, and you had made a sale. Today, the considerations of family, lifestyle, neighborhood, and space may all be secondary to financing. Many new home buyers will buy literally any house if they can just "get onto the ladder."

These days, I (and many other long-time real estate brokers) find that the most important questions may be, "How much will it cost me per month?" and, "What kind of financing can I get?" The financial market has altered the real estate market drastically. There are several ways to finance the purchase of a house. One, of course, is to pay cash, but few can afford that luxury. Most people purchase by making a downpayment to the broker or seller, followed by required monthly mortgage payments of principal, interest, taxes, and property insurance.

Also, the buyer may assume and agree to pay the remaining mortgage debt on your existing mortgage loan. Closing costs will be considerably lower, the interest rate on the old mortgage may be lower than the current rates for a new mortgage, and the transaction can be closed faster.

When placing a contract on a home, the buyer is usually required to make a deposit of 5 to 10 percent of the price as earnest money. The house is then taken off the selling market until approved financing can be arranged. This deposit is forfeited to the seller if the purchaser defaults in carrying out the contract.

When a home purchase is financed through a mortgage loan, the title is passed to the buyer upon closing the sale, but is subject to payments on the mortgage. Failure to make monthly payments when due may result in the lender taking title to the property through legal means such as foreclosure on the mortgage.

How an Interested Buyer Prospects for Mortgage Money

A mortgage is a loan for purchasing a piece of property. The lender supplies cash to buy the house. The mortgagor signs a legal document which obligates and binds him or her to repay the mortgagee in regular installments, including interest, for a specified number of years. The house and lot are pledged as security, and the mortgagor promises to pay the taxes, keep the house insured, and maintain the property in good condition. If the borrower fails to make payments, the lender has the legal right to take over the property, and the borrower may lose any equity.

Savings banks, commercial banks, savings-and-loan associations, mortgage bankers, insurance companies, home sellers, and occasionally relatives make mortgage loans.

Banking and savings-and-loan institutions are usually ready to work with a home buyer. This is their business. Local mortgage brokers and insurance company officials are also possibilities.

If the buyer of your house is a relative or friend, and you are helping with the financing, be sure to keep the deal on a firm business basis—leave nothing to verbal agreement. The fine print is just as important in doing business with someone close as with a stranger or a large, impersonal firm.

Each of the above-named mortgage sources may provide a conventional mortgage loan (without guarantee) or one insured by HUD or guaranteed by the Veterans Administration.

HUD-Insured Financing

A buyer who can qualify and handle the payments on a conventional mortgage, but hasn't enough money for a sizable downpayment, may be able to swing the deal using HUD-insured financing. This allows the borrower to make a smaller downpayment and, frequently, to make lower monthly payments. HUD and FHA have helped thousands of people to buy a first home by guaranteeing the mortgage loan. HUD insurance means that a downpayment may be as little as 5 percent or, in the case of a Veterans Administration guarantee, there may be no downpayment at all. Mortgage insurance has been the backbone of long-term, fixed-rate mortgages.

HUD supports financing for home building, purchase, and

improvement—it does not lend money or build homes; it *insures* mortgages. Under HUD, a home buyer makes a down-payment and obtains a mortgage loan for the balance of the purchase price. The mortgage loan is made by a bank, savings-and-loan association, insurance company, or other lender approved and insured by HUD.

HUD mortgage insurance provides that should the lender have to assign the property or mortgage to them, the agency will pay insurance benefits. HUD will not pay off a loan if a borrower dies.

In the past these mortgages were fixed-rate, long-term loans, paid in monthly installments over a period of several years. Recently HUD has also begun to insure graduated-payment mortgages. The insurance premium—usually one-half of one percent per year on the unpaid balance—is included in the regular monthly mortgage payment to the lender.

To be eligible for HUD insurance, a home buyer must have an acceptable credit record, the cash required for the closing, and enough income to make the monthly payments plus meeting other bills and obligations. HUD also requires that the property—whether old or newly constructed—meet a certain level of standards.

HUD appraises the property to determine the amount of mortgage loan which it will insure. If the lender is willing to make the loan, he or she provides the proper forms for the buyer. The lender then forwards these papers to the nearest HUD field office. If HUD approves the application, the lender and the borrower close the loan. The borrower deals directly with the lender, and the lender handles the transaction with the agency.

HUD Appraisal. These are made solely to determine the maximum mortgage HUD will insure for an acceptable buyer.

HUD does not guarantee the price of the house. If it is new, HUD requires the builder to warrant that it conforms to the specifications upon which the appraisal was made.

Trade and Renovate

If you decide to trade your present house for an older house that needs repairs, it may be possible for you to buy and renovate the second house by obtaining a HUD-insured mortgage loan in an amount that will include the necessary repairs. The HUD commitment will be based on the value of the house as improved.

Creative Financing

There are a number of new, do-it-yourself methods to finance home buying that are meeting the challenge of the new market. These so-called creative financing techniques, while still new in the housing market, are expected to be the norm before too long.

Creative financing takes the money of the buyer and the equity of the seller and arranges a number of ways to sell a house at an initial financing cost lower than the current mortgage interest rate. *Initial* is the key word in many of these creative financing methods. Often, costs accelerate rapidly after the first few years. But the new methods exist for one major reason: lending institutions in this country are no longer willing or able to bear the risks of economic instability and inflation, so in the future these risks will be borne by the homeowner.

The main purpose of all of the many types of creative financing is to get the monthly payments for the purchaser down to an acceptable level, without the seller's being required to substantially reduce the house's sale price. Today's homeowners are finding out that creative financing may be the only way to sell an unwanted house.

The techniques of creative financing can be divided into three categories: the seller's techniques, the bank's techniques, and the builder's techniques.

The new types of loans will help revive lenders battered by an earnings squeeze cause by their large portfolios of old, low-yielding mortgages and their own rising costs of obtaining funds. Though still novelties in the housing market, many of these devices are expected to set the tone for home finance in the future, during good years as well as bad.

The most popular forms of creative financing are: The wrap-around, the balloon, the negative amortizer, the long-term closer, the shared-appreciator, the equity participator, and the graduated-payment, long-term adjustable. Real estate agents estimate that there are at least 100 kinds of new mortgages, and more are being designed every day.

Contract for Deed

A recent, popular method of creative financing that I have often investigated for sellers is the contract for deed, also called a second deed of trust or owner's paper. Here's how it works: The seller offers a house on the market for $100,000. The buyer is willing to assume the existing mortgage of $60,000 at a fixed 10 percent rate of interest. He or she will also make a down-payment of $20,000. This leaves the buyer $20,000 short of the seller's price, but he does not want to get a second mortgage for that amount from the bank.

The seller is anxious to make the sale, and offers to make a contract between himself and the purchaser. The seller allows the buyer to delay payment of the $20,000 for three to five years as long as the buyer pays interest on the money at a rate 3 or 4 percent below current bank rates. Once the moratorium ends, the buyer pays the whole $20,000 in one lump-sum payment, known as a balloon. The result is that the seller gets his or her price and the buyer gets financing for less than the going market rate.

For the purchaser who cannot afford to offer paper, sellers are often willing to accept some form of barter. Potential buyers are offering downpayments with automobiles, mobile homes, precious metals, boats—almost anything of value to avoid paying the high interest rates.

When you have a buyer who needs help financing the purchase of your house, get as complete a credit report on him or her as possible. You should also be thoroughly familiar with your own mortgage and any notes on the property, for there may be limitations or restrictions on your own ability to sell it. For example, there could be a clause that allows the bank to call the entire balance due on the mortgage if you sell the property, or you may not be able to sell without permission from the bank, or there may be a penalty for prepayment of the mortgage.

Undoubtedly you will not be able to assign the mortgage to another party without the consent of the bank.

One common restriction on mortgages allows the bank to call in the mortgage on the sale of the property so that it can charge a higher rate of interest to the new mortgage holder.

Land Contract

It may be possible for you to sell the property on a land contract. Usually, property is transferred when the seller gives the buyer the deed to it. But, under a land contract, the handing over of the deed is delayed until some specified future time.

You will still be the title owner of the property and are liable for the mortgage. The buyer pays you, and, at the future time stipulated, usually when most of the payments have been made, you must deliver the deed to him or her.

Since the property remains yours, restrictive clauses in your mortgage may not apply, but it is absolutely necessary to have any arrangements of this type handled by a competent attorney who is well versed in real estate law.

Assumable Mortgages

Many existing mortgages are at rates far below those of new mortgages. It used to be easy for a buyer to assume such a mortgage simply by paying the seller a sum equal to the seller's equity and taking over the mortgage payments.

You may be able to have a qualified buyer assume your mortgage. Many mortgages have specific clauses disallowing this practice, and banks throughout the country are trying to get laws passed prohibiting it, since they have a great deal of money outstanding in low-interest, long-term loans, which in times of high interest rates are extremely expensive for them to carry.

But if you have an assumable mortgage and it is FHA-insured, it can be assuumed by the buyer making application to the mortgage's loan officer for credit approval. If the approval is forthcoming, you will have no future liability for the note and mortgage. A VA-guaranteed loan can be assumed in the same way, but the buyer, in this case, must himself be eligible for a VA mortgage.

Lenders have recently tried to stop mortgage assumption by enforcing the "due-on-sale" clause included in many contracts. The clause calls for the loan balance to be paid off when the house is sold.

Some banks allow a buyer to assume a mortgage containing a due-on-sale clause if the buyer pays the prevailing mortgage interest rate or, occasionally, a rate slightly below it. While that may save some of the closing costs associated with taking out a new mortgage, it does not provide the benefits of an outright assumption. In many states, however, court decisions or state laws may prevent lenders from enforcing due-on-sale clauses. In those states, buyers may be able to enforce their right to assume a mortgage.

Problems With Private Mortgages

Private mortgages sound like a good solution, but there are pitfalls. All over the country, reports are coming in of difficulties with private home loans. As the notes from the first private mortgages are coming due, some buyers who planned refinancing at lower bank rates are faced with rate levels that are still unaffordable.

Since refinancing is either unavailable or possible only at very high prices, many sellers are starting foreclosure proceedings to get their money out. And there has been a rapidly expanding business in a form of factoring called "discount paper": buying these private mortgages at discounts of as much as 50 percent and more.

One of the difficulties that sellers face with private mortgages is that most banks won't take over the loans for servicing—sending payment notices, etc.—even when they are offered substantial fees.

Another is that lending institutions have not been able to insure these loans. According to one insurance official, "There is a greater possibility of default or claim. The average seller is not trained to evaluate a risk, and when there are late payments, sellers don't know how to follow up and how to collect." Sellers do not have access to credit information that banks do, and often have to take people at their word. However, they are reluctant to get involved in foreclosure proceedings, which take about nine months and cost about $1,200 in legal fees.

Many sellers, unwilling to foreclose, find a solution by continuing to support the loan—rolling over the paper for another five years at a higher interest rate.

Protection for Sellers

A way for the seller to protect himself when holding the second mortgage on the property he has sold is to file a "request for notice of default" with the holder of the first mortgage so that he will be informed if the buyer fails to make payments on an underlying note. If a default of this sort occurs, it will also constitute a default under the second mortgage. Then the seller can cure the default on the first mortgage and start a foreclosure on the second mortgage.

You should get as large a downpayment as possible when offering a second mortgage to ensure that the buyer will risk suffering a substantial loss if he or she defaults.

Other Forms of Creative Financing

Creative financing by lending institutions includes the adjustable-rate mortgage, which moves up and down with the cost of their funds or provides for interest to be renegotiated every few years. About 40 percent of current mortgages are being written this way, a figure that is expected to rise to about 70 percent.

Graduated-Payment Mortgages (Negative Amortizer)

Another version of the bank's adjustable-rate mortgage is the negative-amortization mortgage with graduated payments. The graduated-payment plan allows a reasonable downpayment and lower initial monthly payments in the early years of the loan.

Under the graduated-payment mortgage, payments rise gradually for a set period of years, then level off and remain steady for the balance of the mortgage.

This plan can provide a considerable tax benefit. As with any mortgage program, the interest portion of the monthly payment is tax deductible. And for the first few years of the mortgage, most if not all of the payment is interest.

Under the graduated-payment mortgage the borrower will, in effect, be borrowing additional money during the early years of the mortgage which will be used to reduce the monthly payments. The additional loan is added to the outstanding mortgage payments in later years.

There are five basic plans which vary the rate of monthly payment increases from 2 to 7½ percent, and the number of years over which the payments increase (five or ten years). The greater the rate of increase, or the longer the period of increase, the lower the mortgage payments are in the early years. After a period of five or ten years, depending on which plan is selected, the mortgage payments level off and stay at that level for the remainder of the loan. Graduated-payment mortgage plans increase each year, not each month.

The table below compares the payment schedule of an ordinary FHA-insured loan with the most frequently used of the five graduated-payment mortgage plans. Under the plan shown, mortgage payments would increase 7½ percent each year for five years before leveling off.

Assume that the mortgage amount is $50,000; the interest rate 11½ percent; mortgage insurance premium is 0.5 percent; and the term is thirty years (360 payments).

If prepaid finance charges are 4 percent of the mortgage amount, the annual percentage rate is 9.96 percent for graduated-payment mortgage and 9.96 percent for regular HUD/FHA-insured loans.

MORTGAGE PAYMENT EACH MONTH
(including mortgage insurance premium)

YEAR	Regular HUD/FHA Insured Loan	Graduated-Payment Mortgage Loan
1	$495.50	$379.80
2	$495.50	$408.29
3	$495.50	$438.91
4	$495.50	$471.82
5	$495.50	$507.21
6	$495.50	$545.25
7	$495.50	$545.25
Remaining Payments	$495.50	$545.25

Borrowers taking the negative amortizer are hoping that interest rates will drop and they will be able to refinance later with a conventional mortgage. But if interest rates stay high, the borrower could end up owing a lot more than when he started.

The problem, from the lenders' point of view, is that negative amortization occurs in the early years. They have come up with a way to avoid this through a *pledged-account mortgage,* sometimes called a "flip," for flexible loan insurance plan. Using a flip plan, a portion of the borrower's downpayment is used to set up a savings account. The account is pledged over to the lender and gradually drawn upon to supplement the low monthly payments made by the borrower during the initial years of the loan. The supplements from the savings account typically decline to zero at the end of the fifth year, just at the point when the borrower's out-of-pocket payments—pegged to his or her presumably rising income—rise proportionately.

Adjustable-Rate Mortgage

Although they are no longer granting many conventional thirty-year mortgages, banks and other financial institutions have been active in creative financing. The most familiar of the new alternative mortgages are ones that permit lenders to periodically adjust the rate upward or downward within certain limits. Rate changes are pegged to the cost-of-money index by the federal government. In an adjustable-rate mortgage, monthly payments are tied to prevailing rates. For buyers, it's fine when rates are sliding—and a disaster when they soar.

The variable rate allows lenders to increase the rate by as much as a half percentage point a year, up to a maximum of 2½ points over the life of the loan. A variation, the *renegotiable-rate mortgage,* allows lenders to make larger rate increases but at less frequent intervals. Rates can rise by a maximum of 5 percentage points over the life of the loan.

Shared Appreciation

In this instance, the bank provides a fixed-rate mortgage on bargain terms. But, when the house is sold, it takes a chunk of the price appreciation. In this innovative approach, home buyers might pay an interest rate that is one-third below the prevailing rate and give up one-third of the profit to the lender at the time of sale. The interest rate and the lender's share of appreciation would be left to negotiation, although the lender will probably be limited to no more than 40 percent of the profits.

The major questions about the tax implications of this arrangement have yet to be answered. The payment to the lender may be tax deductible for the borrower. Or, if the Internal Revenue Service takes the position that it is part of the capital gain, borrowers may have to pay tax on profits they never see.

The Wrap-Around Mortgage

Here the seller provides a long-term contract for a deed covering the price of the home less the downpayment. He or she keeps the old, cheap mortgage and charges the buyer a few points more on the contract. Everyone wins, at least over the short term.

Builder's Buy-Down

Creative financing has become an acceptable hedge for home builders, too. The most popular form of builder-provided creative financing involves the builder paying the bank a lump sum in advance to "buy down" or reduce the mortgage rates from an inaccessible 19 percent to, say, 14 percent.

Land Contract

Another popular device is the land contract. The builder will sell the home but not the ground under it. The original sale price of the home ends up being lower since it doesn't include the cost of the plot. The buyer pays rent on the plot permanently or agrees to purchase it outright within twenty years of when he or she buys the home (or another determined time limit).

Barter

If all else fails, for the buyer who can't even afford to offer paper, there is always the option of barter. Current advertisements from potential home buyers offer just about anything—cars, mobile homes, houseboats—as downpayments to help defray the current cost of money.

Comparing Four Mortgages

Assume that the mortgage is on a $100,000 property, with $20,000 down and an $80,000 mortgage at 14 percent for thirty years.

Conventional Mortgage
   Monthly payment: $947.90.

Graduated-Payment Mortgage
   Initial monthly payment is $738.02.
   Maximum monthly payment after six years: $1,059.52.

Renegotiable-Rate Mortgage
   (Maximum interest swing 5 percentage points)
   Initial monthly payment is $947.90.
   Minimum monthly payment after fifteen years: $644.
   Maximum monthly payment after fifteen years: $1,271.20.

Shared-Appreciation Mortgage
   (11 percent after discount)
   Initial monthly payment is $761.86.
   Value of house sold after ten years: $259,373.
   Lender receives $53,124.
   Owner's share: $206,248.

89

(Individual)

117SF

STATUTORY FORM MORTGAGE DEED

of

to secure payment of

with interest payable as provided in a certain promissory note dated

with final maturity on

dollars

grant to

of

with MORTGAGE COVENANTS

(Description and Encumbrances, if any and any additional provisions)

This mortgage is made upon the STATUTORY CONDITION

Signed this   day of   , 19

Witnessed by:

....

....

STATE OF   ⎫
              ⎬ ss.   19
COUNTY OF   ⎭

Personally Appeared
Signer(s) of the foregoing Instrument, and acknowledged the same to be free act and deed, before me.

....
Notary Public / J. of Peace / Commissioner of Superior Court

11

Selling the Extras

Sometimes people get very excited about selling their home. They become caught up in the game—and in dreams of profits. Suddenly it hits them—once their house is sold, they'll have to move.

Panic sets in. Many a possible sale ends there. The repercussions of the sale loom large. Finding a new place to live . . . redecorating . . . painting . . . papering . . . moving . . . buying new furniture . . . selling the old furniture.

Of course, all of the improvements that you have put into your home are a negotiable part of the price you get. This includes such things as carpeting and drapes, as well as the hardware and tracks or rods for drapery. It includes built-in lighting, chandeliers, and bookcases and storage benches; windowseats as well as kitchen equipment and appliances.

In the back and forth negotiations that can occur over the price of a house, extras such as these are useful. Often, they can bring many times their actual value into the price of the house, although you cannot count on getting any more than their replacement might cost the buyer. Do not, however, start dickering over something to which you have emotional attachments. If you think that the dining room chandelier is a treasured family heirloom, take it down before anyone even sees your house and replace it with a fixture that means nothing more to you than dollars and cents.

Once the sale has been completed and you have found a new home, you may find that much or even all of your furniture and other possessions are just not right for it. This is not usually the time to negotiate with the buyer to sell your furniture. If he or she has, throughout your negotiating, expressed a strong interest in buying everything, though, you might put out a feeler. But you will probably get less for furnishings than you would have if you included them in your pre-closing negotiations. There are alternatives.

Garage and Tag Sales

First you must go through everything you have in the house, from old camp trunks in the attic or crawlspace, to those cardboard boxes crammed with junk in the basement. Decide what you want to keep. You may want to walk out clean, or practically clean, keeping only personal items. But don't decide to sell something unless you're sure that you'll have no use for it in your new house. It makes no sense to sell an electric coffeepot or toaster in good condition for a few dollars and then have to replace such an item when you move. What you consider junk, however, might well be worth something to somebody else. There may be objects you'll want to sell because to move or ship them would be too much trouble, even though they'll have to be replaced.

Books, old magazines, and records are heavy and difficult to move around. If you don't want to keep them, you can either mark them individually for sale or take them to a used bookstore in your area. Generally, though, these stores trade this sort of merchandise rather than paying cash. If you decide to include such items in your sale, you can mark nearly new paperbacks in good condition with price tags of 50 cents to a dollar, poor condition, 10 to 35 cents; back-issue magazines can bring either very little or nothing (hold on to them and throw them into a sale, when you and a buyer might be haggling over a price), or a few dollars each (for good-condition old *Life* magazines, for example).

Mark everything with small stick-on price tags, indicating your asking price, although you may have to reduce the price somewhat to make a sale—it's part of the fun of a tag sale.

Higher-priced items such as furniture will not sell as easily as the small appliances and knickknacks that make up most of your sale. You could consider having a professional come into your house to sell the contents, less those items you want to keep. If you have good-quality furniture and *objets d'art,* it might be worth it.

A number of small companies that handle tag and garage sales and auctions have recently sprung up around the country. A professional can advise you on the price that you can reasonably assume you'll receive. Ordinarily, for a percentage of what the sale takes in, one of these services will take care of everything. They will place ads in local papers advertising the sale, put up handbills, mark the merchandise, do the selling, and handle the money. They may be able to get more for the things you want to sell than you could get yourself, but their percentage of profit from the sale will usually be substantial: 25 to 30 percent is not unusual.

If you have the time and energy to put into the sale, all of the proceeds will be yours and the sale itself can be an afternoon of fun. But be sure to check on the laws in your area regarding this kind of sale. Some states require that you charge sales tax and turn sales records and collected taxes over to them.

Make a list of everything in the house that you want to sell, its cost new, how much you want for it, and how much you'll take. Don't leave anything out, even old teaspoons and unmatched glasses. Once you have made the list, you can easily see whether a sale will be worth the time and effort.

List of Tag Sale Items

Item	Asking Price	Selling Price

12

The Closing

This is the moment of truth and, for you, the finale of the sales process. Closing times and dates are scheduled only after all the paperwork has been done.

The buyer has the right to inspect the property just before the closing to be sure that everything agreed to has been left and is in good working order.

All parties with their attorneys meet at the designated time and place to finalize the transfer of ownership. Final closing statements are received and all adjustments are made. You sign, sign, sign, until you think your hand will refuse to move.

Barring any unforeseen difficulties, you will receive your check. Everyone exchanges best wishes and you are happily on your way to the bank. But you must remember, while this is just about the end for you, it is the beginning for the buyer. Buyers should be fully aware of the closing costs connected with buying a home, which typically run between one and 3 percent of the sale price. And there should be, on your part, a full knowledge of the settlement process and settlement costs.

The Real Estate Settlement Procedure Act (RESPA)

Settlement is the formal process by which ownership of real property passes from you to the buyer. It is the end of the home buying process, the time when title to the property is transferred from the seller to the buyer.

RESPA covers most residential mortgage loans used to finance the purchase of a house, a condominium or cooperative apartment unit, a lot with a mobile home, or a lot on which a buyer will build a house or put a mobile home.

RESPA was not designed to set the prices of settlement services. But it provides information to take the mystery out of the settlement process so that you can shop for settlement services and make informed decisions.

The Steps to Take

First, you and the buyer reach an agreement on the price of a house and then sign a sales contract. The terms of the sales contract can be negotiated.

Next, the buyer probably needs a mortgage to finance the purchase. When a buyer files an application for a loan, the lender is required by RESPA to provide a good-faith estimate of the costs of settlement services and a copy of the RESPA information booklet. The lender has three business days, after the written loan application, to mail these materials.

Between loan application time and settlement, there is an opportunity to shop for settlement services.

Then, one business day before settlement, if the bank requests it, the person conducting the settlement must allow an opportunity to see a uniform settlement statement that shows whatever figures are available at that time for settlement charges the buyer is required to pay. At settlement, the completed statement will be given to him or her.

In some parts of the country where there are no actual settlement meetings, or in cases where neither the buyer nor his or her authorized agent attends the closing meeting, the person conducting settlement has the obligation to deliver the statement by mail.

There is no standard settlement process followed in all localities.

Shopping Around

At settlement time, the buyer is committed to the purchase of the property and may have made a partial payment, sometimes called earnest money, to you as the seller. Services may have been performed for which the buyer is obligated to pay. Unless you fail to fulfill a legally binding promise, or have acted fraudulently, the buyer is normally obligated to complete his or her part of the contract and pay settlement costs.

So, the time to decide the terms of sale, raise questions, and establish fair fees is not at the time of settlement services. By the time of settlement, any changes in settlement costs and purchase terms may be difficult to negotiate.

The buyer can also negotiate with you about who pays various settlement fees and other charges. There are generally no fixed rules about which party pays which fees, although in many cases this is largely controlled by local custom.

Among the many factors that determine the amount the buyer will pay for settlement costs are the location of the house, the type of sales contract negotiated, arrangements made with any real estate broker, the lender selected, and the decisions in selecting the various firms that provide required settlement services. If the house is located in a "special flood hazard area," the lender may require flood insurance. Information on flood insurance availability, limits of coverage, and copies of maps can be obtained through the National Flood Insurers Association or from HUD.

Negotiating a Sales Contract

The sales agreement can expressly state which settlement costs the buyer will pay and which costs you will pay, although some may be negotiable up to the time of settlement. Buyers can and do negotiate with sellers as to which party is to pay for specific settlement costs. The success of these negotiations depends on how eager the seller is to sell and the buyer to buy, the quality of the house itself, how long it has been on the market, whether other potential buyers are interested, and how willing each is to negotiate for lower costs. If the contract is silent on these costs, they are still open to negotiation.

There is no standard sales contract that is required. The buyer is entitled to make any modifications or additions in any standard form contract to which you will agree. The following clauses will often be requested by the buyer:

1. As the seller, you provide title, free and clear of all liens and encumbrances except those which the buyer specifically agrees to in the contract or approves when the results of the title search are reported. Who will pay for the title search to determine whether the title is "clear" is negotiable.

2. You or your escrow agent will refund the deposit (earnest money) and cancel the sale if the buyer is unable to secure from a lending institution a first mortgage or deed-of-trust loan with an amount, interest rate, and length of term, as set forth in the contract, within a stated time period.

3. A certificate will be provided at time of settlement, stating that the house is free from termites or termite damage.

4. A certificate will be provided that the plumbing, heating, electrical systems, and appliances are in working order, and that the house is structurally sound. Negotiate who pays for any necessary inspections. There is no uniform custom in most areas. Many buyers prefer to pay for these inspections because they want to know that the inspector is conducting the service for them, not for the seller.

5. An agreement will be reached on how taxes, water, and sewer charges, premiums on existing transferable insurance policies, utility bills, interest on mortgages, and rent (if there are tenants) are to be divided between buyer and seller as of the date of the settlement.

This partial list illustrates the importance of the sales agreement and its terms.

Selecting a Lawyer

Ask the lawyer first what services will be performed for what fee. If the fee seems too high, shop around. Does the attorney have substantial experience in real estate? The U.S. Supreme Court has said that it is illegal for bar associations to fix minimum fee schedules for attorneys, so don't be bashful about discussing and shopping for legal fees you can afford. Your attorney will understand.

Questions you may wish to ask the attorney include: What is the charge for reading documents and giving advice concerning them? For being present at settlement? Will the attorney represent any other party in the transaction? In some areas, attorneys act as closing agents handling the mechanical aspects of the settlement. A lawyer who does this would be representing varied interests.

Choosing a Lender

The buyer's choice of lender will influence not only settlement costs but also whether or not he or she can afford to purchase your house.

Lending institutions require certain settlement services, such as a new survey or title insurance, or they may charge for other settlement-related services, such as the appraisal or credit report. Some other institutions may not have such requirements.

Many lending institutions deal regularly with certain title companies, attorneys, appraisers, surveyors, and others in whom they have confidence. They may want to arrange for settlement services to be provided through these parties.

Questions that the buyer should ask the lender should include:

1. Is he required to carry life or disability insurance? Must he get it from a particular buyer?

2. Is there a late payment charge? How much? How late may the payment be before the charge is imposed?

3. If he wants to pay off the loan in advance of maturity, must a prepayment penalty be paid? How much? If so, for how long a period will it apply?

4. Will the lender release the borrower from personal liability if the loan is assumed by someone else when the house is sold?

5. If the house is sold, and the buyer assumes the loan, will the lender have the right to charge an assumption fee, raise the rate of interest, or require payment in full of the mortgage?

6. If there is a financial emergency, will the terms of the loan include a future advances clause, permitting a loan of additional money on the mortgage after part of the original loan has been paid?

7. Must money be paid into a special reserve (escrow or im-

pound) account to cover taxes or insurance? If so, how large a deposit will be required at the closing of the sale? The amount of reserve deposits required is limited under RESPA. Some recent state laws have required that these accounts bear interest for the benefit of the buyer.

8. The FHA, VA, and Farmers Home Administration loans involve federal ceilings on permissible charges for some settlement services.

Choosing the Settlement Agent

Settlement practices vary from one place to another, even within the same county or city. In various areas, settlements are conducted by lending institutions, title insurance companies, escrow companies, real estate brokers, and attorneys for the buyer or seller.

Title Services

A title search may take the form of an abstract—a compilation of pertinent legal documents which provides a condensed history of the property ownership and related matters. In many areas, title searches are performed by extracting information from the public record without assembling abstracts. In either situation, an expert examination is necessary to determine the status of title, and this is normally made by attorneys or title company employees.

In areas where both title insurance companies and attorneys perform these and other settlement services, compare fees for services (such as title certification, document preparation, notary fee, closing fee, and so on) provided by each to determine the better source for these services.

In many jurisdictions, a few days or weeks before settlement the title insurance company will issue a binder (sometimes called a commitment to insure) or preliminary report—a summary of findings based on the search or abstract. It is usually sent to the lender for use until the title insurance policy is issued after the settlement. The binder lists all the defects in, and liens against, the title identified by the search.

Title insurance is often required to protect the lender against loss if a flaw in title is not found by the title search made when the house is purchased. In some states, attorneys provide bar-related title insurance as part of their services in examining title and providing a title opinion. In these states, the attorney's fee may include the title insurance premium, although the total title-related charges in the transaction should be taken into account.

A title insurance policy issued only to the lender does not protect the buyer. Nor does a policy issued to the seller protect the buyer. To protect himself from loss because of a mistake made by the title searcher, or because of a legal defect of a type which does not appear on the public records, the buyer will need an owner's policy. Such a mistake rarely occurs, but when it does, it can be financially devastating to the uninsured. An owner's policy is usually much less expensive if purchased simultaneously with a lender's policy.

Depending upon practice in the jurisdiction, there may be no need for a full historical title search each time the title to a home is transferred. If your home has changed hands within the last several years, the new buyer may get a "reissue rate" from the title company that issued the previous title insurance policy, which would be a lower charge than for a new policy.

If your title insurance policy is available, the buyer should take it to the title insurer or lawyer selected for the search.

To mark the boundaries of the property as set out in the title, lenders may require a survey. A home buyer may be able to avoid the cost of a repetitive complete survey of the property if the surveyor who previously surveyed the project can be located. He or she can update the existing survey. However, the requirements of investors who buy loans originated by the lender may limit the lender's discretion to negotiate this point.

What the Buyer Will Receive Before Settlement

The lender is required by the terms of RESPA to give the borrower his good-faith estimate based upon his experience in the locality in which the property is located, for each settlement charge that he anticipates will be paid, except for paid-in-advance hazard insurance premium and reserves deposited with the lender. The estimate may be stated as either a dollar amount or range for each charge. Where the lender designates the use of a particular firm, the lender must make its good-faith estimate based upon his knowledge of the amounts charged by the firm.

The form used for this estimate must be concise and clear, and the estimates must bear a reasonable relationship to the costs that will likely be incurred. If the lender provides estimates in the form of ranges, he or she should provide information on what the total settlement costs will most likely be.

Lenders are not required to give good-faith estimates for reserves deposited with them, or for the prepaid hazard insurance premium, because these charges require information not normally known to the lender at the time of loan application.

The lender should tell the buyer what his policies are in terms of reserve accounts, for which items the lender requires reserves, and for what period of time.

Some assumptions may be necessary to get an idea of the costs at closing; for example, the assessed value of the property for determining property taxes. The lender can probably be more specific on hazard insurance premiums, particularly for those coverages which a lender requires.

The final costs may not be the same as the estimates. Estimates are subject to changing market conditions, and fees may change. Changes in the date of settlement may result in changes in escrow and proration requirements. In certain cases, it may not be possible for the lender to anticipate exactly the pricing policies of settlement firms. The lender's estimate is not a guarantee.

Lender Designations

Some lending institutions follow the practice of designating specific settlement service providers to be used for legal services, title examination, title insurance, or the conduct of settlement.

Where this occurs the lender, under RESPA, is required to provide a statement setting forth:

1. The name, address, and telephone number of each designated provider. This must include a statement of the specific service each designated firm is to provide, as well as an estimate of the cost for the service, based on the lender's previous experience with the provider.

2. Whether each designated firm has a business relationship with the lender.

While designated firms often provide the services needed, a conflict of interest may exist. Contact other firms to determine whether their costs are competitive and their services comparable.

Disclosure of Settlement Costs One Day Before Closing and Delivery

One business day before settlement, the buyer has the right to inspect the form, called the uniform settlement statement, on which are itemized the services provided and the fees charged. This form is filled out by the person who will conduct the settlement meeting. Be sure to have the name, address, and telephone number of the settlement agent.

The settlement agent may not have all costs available the day before closing, but he or she is obligated to show, upon request, what is available.

The uniform settlement statement must be delivered or mailed to both you and the buyer at or before settlement. If that right is waived, however, the completed statement will be mailed at the earliest practicable date.

In parts of the country where the settlement agent does not require a meeting, or where you do not attend the settlement, the statement will be mailed as soon as practicable after settlement and no advance inspection is required.

The uniform settlement statement is not used in situations where:

1. There are no settlement fees charged to the buyer (because you have assumed all settlement-related expenses).

2. The total amount the borrower is required to pay for all charges imposed at settlement is determined by a fixed amount, and the borrower is informed of this fixed amount at the time of loan application. In the latter case, the lender is required to provide the borrower, within three business days of application, an itemized list of services rendered.

Escrow Closing

Settlement practices differ from state to state. In some parts of the country, settlement may be conducted by an escrow agent, which may be a lender, real estate agent, title company representative, attorney, or an escrow company. After entering into a contract of sale, you and the buyer sign an escrow agreement which requires you to deposit specified documents and funds with the agent.

Unlike other types of closing, the parties do not meet around a table to sign and exchange documents. The agent may request a title report and policy; draft a deed or other documents; obtain rent settlements; pay off existing loans; adjust taxes, rents, and insurance between the buyer and seller; compute interest on loans; and acquire hazard insurance. All this may be authorized in the escrow agreement. If all the papers and monies are deposited with the agent within the agreed time, the escrow is "closed."

The escrow agent then records the appropriate documents and gives each party the documents and money each is entitled to, including the completed uniform settlement statement. If one party has failed to fulfill his or her agreement, the escrow is not closed and legal complications may follow.

Title Companies. Under the law, you may not require, as a condition of sale, that title insurance be purchased by the buyer from any particular title company. A violation of this will make you liable in an amount equal to three times all charges made for the title insurance.

Specific Settlement Services

The following defines and discusses each specific settlement service.

Sales/Broker's Commission

This is the total dollar amount of sales commission, usually paid by the seller. Fees are usually a percentage of the selling price of the house, and are intended to compensate brokers or salespersons for their services. Custom and/or the negotiated agreement between you and the broker determines the amount of the commission.

Division of Commission

If several brokers or salespersons work together to sell the house, the commission may be split among them.

Commission Paid at Settlement

Sometimes the broker will retain the earnest money deposit to apply towards his or her commission.

Items Payable in Connection with Loan

These are the fees which lenders charge to process, approve, and make the mortgage loan.

Loan Origination

This fee covers the lender's administrative costs in processing the loan. Often expressed as a percentage of the loan, the fee will vary among lenders and from locality to locality. Generally, the buyer pays the fee unless another arrangement has been made with the seller and written into the sales contract.

Loan Discount

Often called "points," a loan discount is a one-time charge used to adjust the yield on the loan to what market conditions demand. It is used to offset constraints placed on the yield by state or federal regulations. Each "point" is equal to one percent of the mortgage amount. For example, if a lender charges four points on a $30,000 loan this amounts to a charge of $1,200.

Appraisal Fee

This charge, which may vary significantly from transaction to transaction, pays for a statement of property value for the lender, made by an independent appraiser or by a member of the lender's staff. The lender needs to know if the value of the property is sufficient to secure the loan according to the provision of the mortgage contract, and if the lender must foreclose and take title to the house.

The appraiser inspects the house and the neighborhood and considers sales prices of comparable houses and other factors in determining its value. The appraisal report may contain photos and other information. It will provide the factual data upon which the appraiser based the appraised value.

The appraisal fee may be paid by either you or the buyer, as agreed in the sales contract. In some cases, this fee is included in the mortgage insurance application.

Credit Report Fee

This fee covers the cost of the credit report, which shows how the buyer has handled other credit transactions. The lender uses this report in conjunction with information about the buyer submitted with the application regarding income, outstanding bills, and employment.

Lender's Inspection Fee

This charge covers inspections, often of newly constructed housing, made by personnel of the lending institution or an outside inspector.

Mortgage Insurance Application Fee

This fee covers processing the application for private mortgage insurance, which may be required on certain loans. It may cover both the appraisal and application fee.

Assumption Fee

This fee is charged for processing papers for cases in which the buyer takes over your payments on a prior loan.

Items Required by Lender to be Paid in Advance

Certain items may have to be prepaid, such as interest, mortgage insurance premium and hazard insurance premium, at the time of settlement.

Interest

Lenders usually require that at settlement borrowers pay the interest that accrues on the mortgage from the date of settlement to the beginning of the period covered by the first monthly payment. For example, suppose the settlement takes place on May 15, and your first regular monthly payment will be due July 1, to cover charges for the month of June. On the settlement date, the lender will collect interest for the period from May 15 to June 1.

Mortgage Insurance Premium

Mortgage insurance protects the lender from loss due to payment default by the homeowner. The first payment is often due on the day of settlement. The premium may cover a specific number of months or a year in advance. With this insurance protection, the lender is willing to make a larger loan, reducing the downpayment requirements. This type of insurance should not be confused with mortgage life, credit life, or disability insurance designed to pay off a mortgage in the event of physical disability or death of the borrower.

Hazard Insurance Premium

This premium prepayment is for insurance protection against loss due to fire, windstorm, and natural hazards. This coverage may be included in a homeowner's policy, which insures against additional risks that may include personal liability and theft. Lenders often require payment of the first year's premium at settlement.

A hazard insurance or homeowner's policy may not protect against loss caused by flooding. In special flood-prone areas identified by HUD, federal law may require a flood insurance policy. This insurance can be bought at low, federally subsidized rates in participating communities under the National Flood Insurance Act.

Reserves Deposited with Lenders

Reserves (sometimes called "escrow" or "impound" accounts) are funds held in an account by the lender to assure future payment for such recurring items as real estate taxes and hazard insurance.

Mortgage Insurance

The lender may require that part of the total annual premium be placed in the reserve account at settlement. The portion to be placed in reserve may be negotiable.

City/County Property Taxes

The lender may require a regular monthly payment to the reserve account for property taxes.

Annual Assessments

This reserve item covers assessments that may be imposed by subdivisions or municipalities for special improvements (such as sidewalks, sewers, or paving) or fees (such as homeowners association fees).

Title Charges

Title charges may cover a variety of services performed by the lender or others for handling and supervising the settlement transaction and related services.

113

Settlement or Closing Fee

This fee is paid to the settlement agent. Responsibility for payment of this fee should be negotiated between you and the buyer when the sales contract is signed.

Abstract or Title Search, Title Examination, Title Insurance Binder

These charges cover the costs of the search and examination of previous ownership, transfers, and so on, to determine whether you can convey clear title to the property, and to disclose any matters on record that could adversely affect the buyer or the lender.

Examples of title problems are unpaid mortgages, judgment of tax liens, conveyances of mineral rights, leases, and power line easements or road right-of-ways that could limit use and enjoyment of the real estate. In some areas, a title insurance binder is called a commitment to insure.

Document Preparation

There may be a separate document fee that covers preparation of final legal papers, such as a mortgage, deed of trust, note, or deed.

Notary Fee

This fee is charged for the cost of having a licensed person affix his or her name and seal to various documents authenticating the execution of these documents by the parties.

Attorney's Fees

You and the buyer may each retain an attorney to check the various documents and to represent you at all stages of the transaction including settlement.

Title Insurance

The total cost of owner's and lender's title insurance; the borrower may pay all, a part, or none of this cost depending on the terms of the sales contract or local custom.

Lender's Title Insurance

A one-time premium may be charged at settlement for a lender's title policy which protects the lender against loss due to problems or defects in connection with the title. The insurance is usually written for the amount of the mortgage loan and covers losses due to defects or problems not identified by the title search and examination. In most areas this is customarily paid by the borrower unless the seller agrees in the sales contract to pay part or all of it.

Owner's Title Insurance

This charge is for owner's title insurance protection and protects against losses due to title defects. In some areas, it is customary for you to provide the buyer with an owner's policy and pay for this policy. In other areas, if the buyer desires an owner's policy, he must pay for it.

THE REAL ESTATE BROKER'S GUIDE

Government Recording and Transfer Charges

These fees may be paid either by you or the buyer, depending upon the contract. The buyer usually pays the fees for legally recording the new deed and mortgage. These fees, collected when property changes hands or when a mortgage loan is made, may be quite large and are set by state and/or local governments. City, county, and/or state tax stamps may have to be purchased as well.

Additional Settlement Charges: Survey

The lender or the title insurance company may require that a surveyor conduct a property survey to determine the exact location of the house and the lot line, as well as easements and rights of way. This is a protection for the buyer as well. Usually the buyer pays the surveyor's fees, but sometimes the seller pays.

Pest and Other Inspections

This fee covers inspections for termite or other pest infestation. This may be important if, in the sales contract, you promised to transfer the property free from pests or pest-caused damage. This fee can be paid either by you or the buyer, depending upon the terms of the sales contract. Lenders vary in their requirements as to such an inspection.

REAL ESTATE CLOSING—STATEMENT OF ADJUSTMENTS

FILE NO. _____

SELLER _____

BUYER _____

LOCATION _____

DATE _____ Adjustments as of_____

==

CREDITS DUE TO THE SELLER(S)

Purchase Price Per Contract:_____ $

Taxes: List_____ Total Tax for Year _____
        Paid to_____ months _____ days

Fuel Oil:_____

Water:_____

Other:_____

_____

                Total Amount Due Seller(s) $_____

==

CREDITS DUE TO THE BUYER(S)

Deposit per Contract:_____ $

Mortgage Pay-Off:_____

_____

Water:_____

Rent:_____

Taxes:_____

Other:_____

_____

Balance due Seller(s)   Cash to Balance $_____
                             Total $_____

==

STATEMENT TO SELLER

Cash to Balance_____ $_____

Less:

    Conveyance tax_____

    Legal Fees_____

    Recording fee_____

    Broker Commission_____

    Miscellaneous Disbursements_____

    Mortgage Pay-Off_____

    _____

    _____

    _____

    _____

Other_____

    _____

Net Cash Due to Seller $_____

Plus Deposit (if in escrow) $_____

$_____

_____
                  Seller

_____
                  Seller

13

Condos and Co-ops

The market for condominiums and cooperatives, rare things a decade ago, has soared throughout the country. There are today about 1½ million apartments and town houses in the condo/co-op market, and that number could double in the next five years. In New York City, a record number of apartment rentals are converting to the co-op plan. In Florida, California, Arizona, condos are everywhere. Eleven percent of all home purchases in 1979 were condos (in most parts of the country, the more popular of the two plans).

Condos and co-ops are the hottest sector of the real estate market right now. High prices and higher interest rates have made buying many one-family houses impossible for most new home buyers. The smaller condos and co-ops are cheaper to buy and cheaper to keep up.

You don't have all the time-consuming responsibilities that you have with a single-family house. No more mowing the lawn, shoveling snow, cleaning the pool, painting the exterior. You take care of your own apartment and maintenance staff takes care of the rest.

Today's smaller families also make larger quarters generally uneconomical. In 1960 the average household was made up of

3.33 people; in 1980 that number had dropped to 2.75. Condos and co-ops are particularly designed for smaller families, for retired people, and for singles.

But what makes co-ops and condos more desirable than rental property? Investment potential. Both co-ops and condominiums have proved excellent investments. They are not like traditional real estate investments in land and houses and may be more susceptible to market fluctuations, but they have performed very well compared with the real estate market as a whole.

Cooperatives

When you buy or sell a co-op, you make a stock transaction. On paper, you don't sell an apartment, but rather shares of stock in a corporation that happens to be a building. And you don't have a deed in your safe deposit box, but a stock certificate.

The number of shares you have usually depends on the size and location of your apartment in the building or building complex. For example, for a building with fifty apartments of equal size and location, the cooperative might issue 10,000 shares—200 for each apartment. In practice, apartments would not be exactly equal, so a space with an extra closet might have 210 shares, while the apartment with a view of the back wall of the building next door would have 190. The number of shares you own determines your vote in the apartment corporation and forms the basis of your monthly maintenance payment.

Monthly maintenance payments are made up of the building's operating expenses, property taxes, and mortgage payments. Your share of these is spelled out in a proprietary lease which gives shareholders the exclusive right to occupy apartments. After the initial issue, the price of shares in the cooperative is generally *not* governed by the co-op board, but by the marketplace.

The most active co-op market in the country has been for the past decade in New York City, specifically in the borough of Manhattan. Since the vacancy rate in rental apartments has been running at less than 3 percent, co-ops have been an important alternative. And, even though there has been a recent softening of the market, prices of cooperative apartments have shot up as much as 1,000 percent over the past years.

A family I know (I sold their house when they moved to their apartment) bought a six-room apartment in a landmark New York building during the last slump in the co-op market in 1976. They paid $80,000. Last year, they were offered over $600,000 for the apartment.

Some people who didn't buy at the market's low point have also been able to see a substantial appreciation of their apartment's market value. Last year a friend for whom I had found a rural summer residence was offered a short-term deal to buy the five-room apartment where he lives for an "insider's" price of $90,000. He decided not to buy, and he still lives in the apartment at his old rent. The only difference is that the co-op committee is his new landlord—but if he now decides to buy the apartment, the new purchase price is $225,000.

A co-op corporation can be formed by a number of tenants already residing in a building or by a realtor who sees a profitable short-term investment: he or she will (at its simplest) buy the building, set up a cooperative corporation, make some repairs, make an offering, sell the apartments at a profit, and have the apartment owners take over the cooperative corporation.

Generally, the corporation buys the entire piece of property in a single transaction. The project is financed by selling stock plus a blanket mortgage loan. The loan installments are paid by the shareholders' monthly maintenance payments.

The co-op is often formed by a sponsoring group which has done the necessary groundwork to develop the cooperative and the space it will occupy. The units can be in detached, semidetached, row house, or multifamily buildings.

The cooperative can either buy the land and contract for construction of the housing or it can buy a complete project from an existing owner or from a real estate investor who has built the project for sale to a cooperative.

There has been a steady conversion of rentals to co-ops during the past few years and, particularly where there is a shortage of good available housing, it has been tenant groups that have been the guiding force. The tenants in this kind of arrangement initiate the co-op plan and make the terms that best fit their own particular needs. By eliminating the middleman's profit, many tenants are able to purchase apartments at great savings. Tenant-sponsored co-op plans have been relatively scarce, but we may be seeing more of them in the future.

But there are often rules that govern the co-oping of buildings so that the statutory tenants cannot be summarily tossed out on their collective ears. New York State has a few different plans which allow co-oping with as few as 35 percent of the tenants agreeing.

A HUD/FHA-insured mortgage may be used to build new housing or to acquire and rehabilitate existing structures for conversion to co-op ownership. HUD/FHA also gives technical advice and help to co-ops in organizing the corporation and in planning, building, and operating.

Selling Points for Co-ops

A co-op offers the same kind of advantages as condominiums and owning your own home. You don't have to worry about arbitrary rent increases and you get certain tax benefits and equity buildup. You can also make any changes you want without worrying about lease restrictions. One special selling point is that a prospective buyer doesn't sign his or her name to a mortgage when buying into a co-op. There are no closing costs other than lawyers' fees and a transfer fee paid when the lease is signed.

Other important advantages and selling points for a prospective buyer are:

Protection Against Rising Costs. Co-ops operate on a non-profit basis, so the owners pay only their share of the actual operating costs. Increases in costs are limited to actual increases of operation. In rental housing, rent is often affected by supply and demand. So, during times of housing shortages and rising costs, rents may soar, even though the landlord's operating costs may not have been significantly increased.

Tax Advantages. A co-op owner has basically the same income tax advantages as a conventional homeowner. You can deduct from your income for federal (and sometimes state) income tax your share of the real estate taxes and mortgage interest that the co-op paid during the year.

Absence of Landlord's Profit. Because the owners are their own landlord, and since they operate on a nonprofit basis, their monthly housing cost does not include an allocation for landlord's profit. This in itself may amount to a reduction of 10 percent or more in monthly costs.

Reduced Maintenance Expense. People tend to take better care of property they own. Maintenance costs are therefore usually less in a co-op than in a rental building.

123

Equity Accruals. If a co-op is operated successfully, you can look forward to accruing substantial equity when you decide to sell, just as you can with any form of home ownership.

Mortgages and Maintenance

A co-op mortgage covers the entire project, and all the shareholders are liable together. This means that a mortgage foreclosure cannot be brought against any one owner. If any owner fails to make his monthly payment, everyone else has to make up his or her share. This is one of the main reasons why co-op boards are so selective about the financial background of new buyers.

Downpayments are based on the difference between the total cost of the project and the mortgage, plus working capital. The amount of the downpayment varies with the cost of the project and the sizes and types of the apartments.

Each member of the cooperative signs an occupancy agreement similar to a lease. Once you sign, you agree to pay the cooperative a monthly carrying charge equal to your share of the money that the co-op needs to meet its expenses. The agreement states which repairs and maintenance the co-op will handle and which are your responsibility.

Operating costs vary from time to time. When this happens, the monthly carrying charges paid by members may be adjusted up or down to reflect such changes.

Co-op Boards

The board of directors of a cooperative decide everything that concerns the management and maintenance of the project, but the management must meet standards of the lender, and of HUD/FHA if the mortgage is HUD-insured.

Co-ops are almost universally more restrictive than condos. Even though boards are not permitted to violate civil rights laws, they can reject anyone whose financial assets don't seem to match the standards of the building. This gives the board a lot of latitude in approving buyers, and it's difficult to sort out what may or may not be discriminatory. Co-op boards have also rejected buyers whose lifestyle threatens to mar domestic peace and quiet—including rock stars, actors, and even former presidents of the United States.

Absentee ownership is discouraged by co-op boards, although it isn't too difficult to overcome the restriction. A general rule is that co-op owners may lease their unit for only two years, and the tenant is subject to approval by the board.

Selling Your Co-op

All of the advantages that induced you to buy your co-op in the first place can be used as prime selling points when you are ready to sell. Even so, selling a co-op can sometimes be difficult. It can be a problem to find a buyer who is willing to accept the terms of the existing mortgage. You can't remove the mortgage on your cooperative apartment as you can with a condominium. If the buyer you find needs financing, he or she will have to look for a second mortgage, putting up the stock in the co-op as security. One problem with this is that many co-ops do not allow it.

It has been difficult for individuals to get even expensive mortgages for co-op purchases. In New York City, for example, many cooperative corporations require a minimum downpayment of 50 percent, and in some instances no outside financing is permitted. Only recently has the Federal Home Loan Bank Board authorized federal savings and loans associations to make co-op loans at all.

The board of directors reserves the right to approve any new buyer. It is not enough for you to find a buyer. That person or family must be fully approved by the board, which may involve a lot of waiting and anxiety for your buyer. On the one hand, the screening system is an advantage for the other shareholders since it helps protect them against a new owner who might not be able to keep up his or her financial interest. But it can be a problem for you when you sell.

The cooperative has a thirty-day option to purchase the shares of any shareholder who wants to withdraw. If the co-op does not act on the option, then you can usually begin to sell your apartment on the open market. Still, any new shareholder must be approved by the cooperative. Subletting or renting on a short-term basis is allowed under certain circumstances. But in most cases, long-term occupancy is restricted to shareholders in the corporation.

Condominiums

Condominiums take many forms, from towering inner-city structures to suburban town houses with beautiful, environmentally designed surroundings, to beach resort and retirement apartments. Some are conversions of luxurious old rental structures which have been rehabilitated and modernized into highly desirable dwellings. Some, however, are merely old, exhausted rental properties which have been painted, carpeted, given new kitchen equipment, and thrown onto the condominium market. Condominium laws can be applied to any of these properties.

The price of an individual condo depends upon the structure as a whole, as well as on the value of all the other units.

Condominiums are created under a special real estate law in the state where they are located. The laws differ in detail from state to state, and documents differ from one development to another.

Financing New Condos

As opposed to co-ops, condominiums are real estate. You receive a deed for your apartment or house and pay taxes just as you would on any property. As an owner you are automatically a voting member of the condominium association.

A builder or developer usually finances a condominium and then sells the individual units, each buyer arranging his or her own financing. Mortgage loans are generally more available for condos than for co-ops. Buyers often form an association to manage the property, but this has nothing to do with purchase transactions.

Taxes and Other Basic Expenses

In a condominium, any taxes and special assessments must be levied against each individual unit separately rather than against the condominium as a whole. And each unit must carry its own mortgage. Therefore, your title is not endangered if other owners fail to meet their mortgage and real estate tax payments. And you have no responsibility for deficiencies in these payments.

As a condominium owner you have the same tax advantages as a conventional homeowner. You may deduct real estate taxes and mortgage interest from your federal income tax.

Management

Both condos and co-ops are nonprofit corporations run by a board which is periodically elected from among the residents.

127

The board is involved in everything that affects the property as a whole, including insurance and maintenance. It holds elections and issues periodic financial reports. It also sets policy on the sale of individual units and use of all common areas.

Most condo boards allow buyers to purchase an apartment for investment and rent it to someone else. This has created a transient quality in some condominiums. In most instances, boards also reserve the right to approve new buyers.

House rules are specific in both co-ops and condos and, depending on the development or building, they can be quite strict. For example, retirement communities frequently restrict pets and limit the number of children that can visit at any one time. The rules and regulations of day-to-day living are extremely important factors, and when you sell your condominium or cooperative you also have to sell the rules that go with it. Most owners take the rules very seriously, and most boards have spent long hours working out plans that satisfy as many tenants as possible. Any prospective buyer is going to have to be able to live with the plan that has been set out for all the owners.

Owner's Rights

Owners have certain rights over and above the average renter. Merely by running for office on the board of directors, you can take on an active role in the condominium association. At the minimum, you can participate in the meetings and vote on issues that directly affect your day-to-day living conditions. You, with others, can change things. Those who live in rental buildings rarely have a similar opportunity. The extent of your interest and the interest of other owners is the true measure of a successful condominium.

Selling Your Condo

The market in condominiums is newer than the housing market as a whole, and has characteristics different from the general market for other kinds of housing. Even though inflation has made substantial paper profits possible throughout the condominium market, there has not been extensive profit taking.

One reason for this could be the ease with which owners can rent their apartments, particularly in resort areas, and realize a profit without sacrificing ownership.

As an owner in a condominium you may either have a mortgage or own your property free and clear. Mortgage payments are your own responsibility. Since there is individual title to each unit, you can place mortgages or remove them, regardless of what your neighbors do. If you own a condominium, you can offer a prospective buyer title to your unit free and clear or you may offer mortgage financing on any terms you wish. You can sell your condo unit in exactly the same way that you would sell a house—through real estate agents or directly.

Anyone who might be a prospective buyer for your condominium will want to read all the documents pertaining to it and learn whether any amendments have been made or proposed. You should be sure that everything is in order, and before you put your condo on the market, check all possible problem areas, just as any homeowner should check all deeds, insurance papers, and so on.

A declaration normally provides for a master hazard-insurance policy against loss by fire and other perils. This policy should contain a condominium property endorsement which recognizes that condos have a multiple number of beneficiaries. You should make sure that this sort of endorsement is part of your insurance package.

There should be sufficient liability coverage for the entire development. Check to be sure that the liability insurance policy names, as insured, the board of directors and each owner individually.

Through the board of directors, you should be able to find out if the condominium development will be expanded beyond current building levels, if more land or condominium or rental units are planned, and if the developer's right to expand the complex is outlined in the declaration.

You should also discover the extent of any other control by the developer, before and after the condominium has been legally constituted, and the effect on the developer's future rights and obligations. Some condominium developers retain ownership of parts of a project, usually the recreational facilities and sometimes the land, and lease them back to the buyers for ninety-nine years. It's important for you to know the difference between full ownership (fee simple title), which gives the owners control of the common area, and a leasehold, which gives the lessee full control over the property.

Be sure you know the boundaries of your individual condominium unit and the boundaries of the common estate. Also, whether there are restricted common areas.

Spell out to what degree transient occupancy is allowed. Some mortgages specify that a family unit cannot be rented for transient or hotel purposes (a rental less than thirty days or any rental that provides customary hotel services). Owners of individual units should have the right to lease, subject to the restrictions of the declaration and bylaws.

To be sure of a good title, free and clear of any liens, it is a good idea to buy an owner's title policy. Make sure you fully inform any prospective buyer about restrictions on rights to resell. Can your condominium unit be sold on the open market or must it first be offered to the association for a particular period of time?

The association may reserve the right to clear prospective buyers before they are permitted to buy. This would contradict "fee simple ownership," which carries with it the undisputed right of disposal. While "right of first refusal" is not prohibited in some state statutes, it is specifically prohibited in condos which have HUD-insured mortgages.

Selling the Older Condo

In addition to all of the above information, a prospect ready to buy your older condo will want to know about the financial performance of the condominium itself over the past few years. You should be ready to provide a current budget and recent, audited financial statement. The income statement (or statement of profit or loss) will show actual income and expenses for the past year. A prospective buyer will want to compare this statement with the budget for the current year. Another part of the financial statement, the balance sheet, will show assets and liabilities—how much money is in the bank or invested, how much is owed to the association by the owners (accounts receivable), and how much is owed by the association to others (accounts payable).

If accounts receivable is a large amount, it may show that the owners are behind in paying their assessments. If accounts payable are high, it may indicate that the association has trouble paying its bills on time. Neither situation is a good one, and may present negotiating problems. You should be well informed and ready to answer any questions.

Special Assessments. Because the budget may not show whether a special assessment is planned for the next year or

131

two, a prospective buyer may ask about any actual or proposed special assessments. Sometimes special assessments for major repairs and improvements can be extremely high and a new owner will have to pay for it. Have this information available.

Lawsuits. You should be aware whether or not any lawsuits involving the association are pending or planned.

Some types of litigation are routine. But if there are many of them, or if there is a major suit, it may mean the community is embroiled in bitter actions that could carry over from the courts to everyday living in the building. While negative results in any of these areas can hurt your chances to sell at your price, positive results greatly enhance the value of the condo. Each item is a selling point.

You should provide buyers with the House Rules or other regulations. Some rules are necessary to live in close proximity with other families. They are vital selling points and can help attract prospective buyers. The rules governing items such as noise, pets, parking, pool use, children visiting, and so on, will appeal to some buyers and put off others. Part of your sales plan should be to find a buyer who not only likes your unit, but also likes the way the building is run.

Maintenance and Operation. A prospective buyer is going to look around for signs that the condominium is well maintained and that the owners are proud to live there. You don't have much control over the impression the condominium gives unless you are on the board. You cannot hide the need for repairs, and you cannot hide poorly kept grounds or uncollected litter.

If there are problems in the environment of the condominium, they will pull down your asking price. But if it is well kept and prosperous looking, it will help carry your asking price.

Other Important Questions. Are your dues paid up? You should have a certificate signed by the managing agent or an officer of the association showing that you are fully paid. A new owner may become liable for any dues that you fail to meet.

Has the association approved any improvements you have made in your unit? Most associations require that an owner obtain permission before making any changes on the outside of the unit or interior changes that affect the structure of the building. Even installing new locks or a washing machine may require approval. A prospective buyer may ask for written proof that any improvements requiring approval have been okayed. If they haven't, your buyer may be required to remove unauthorized improvements at his or her own expense.

In some states, new buyers are entitled to a special "resale certificate" answering many of these questions. If this is a regulation in your state, be ready to supply the correct information. It will save problems and misunderstandings in the long run.

Advantages and Disadvantages of Co-ops and Condos

In recent years, condos and co-ops have generally proved to be good investments. Prices have risen steadily in both kinds of housing, and owners have just about as much control over expenses as owners of one-family houses.

There are some disadvantages. One person's assets are frequently another's liabilities. Condos and co-ops are small, sometimes too small for comfort. And they demand, as their name implies, cooperative living. This means that owners have to be willing to work with their neighbors. Condo and co-op living is vastly different from rental living in this regard. In a rental apartment you might live next door to someone for years and never meet him. Not so in a condo and co-op. You and your neighbors have mutual interests and mutual investments to protect. Together, condo owners have to reach agreements about the financial, aesthetic, and social life of the building or group of buildings in which they live. These decisions do not always match individual feelings and choices. They also can interfere with selling individual condos.

Both condominiums and cooperatives are forms of common ownership. Both give you exclusive use of a unit in a building or group of buildings. And both have communal areas—hallways, elevators, parking lots, recreation rooms, swimming pools, and so on—that are shared by the owners. Condos are the more popular of the two, outnumbering co-ops three to one. Primarily this is because condo rules and regulations are simpler and easier to comply with than the more rigid co-ops. It's easier to buy and sell, and there is less interference from the other owners and fewer restrictions on the occupants. The owner of a condo owns the unit outright. The owner of a co-op owns a share of the corporation that owns the actual real estate.

Converting Rentals

Much of the recent growth of the condo and co-op market we have seen has been in converted rental apartments. This process has been so profitable for both owners and buyers that conversions are multiplying at an unprecedented rate. And prices have climbed rapidly to match the demand. Owners of prime buildings, in these days of high costs and inflated dollars, can make much more by converting than by renting in the usual way. Tenants of buildings that "go co-op" are usually willing to buy because they can purchase their apartment below the market level. Buyers usually realize a large capital gain literally overnight, at least on paper, and they don't have to move.

As profitable as it is, few conversions go off smoothly. Not everyone can afford to buy, even at an inside price. Many tenants find that the high interest rates preclude getting a mortgage. In some buildings, maintenance fees plus mortgage payments double what the tenant was paying in rent.

A building conversion can be a serious problem for tenants who cannot—or choose not—to buy. Depending on the conversion plan adopted, they may be forced to move or into a higher rent bracket.

Although tenants in a converting building sometimes protest vigorously, there are few laws that govern the process. According to a recent study of cities in which several conversions had already occurred, fewer than one in five had such laws. A few had created special rules to protect the elderly and handicapped from eviction from converting buildings, and a few had temporarily halted new conversions.

Tension between factions is common in buildings that are in the process of converting. The present owner, the tenants who want to buy, and the tenants who don't want to buy, all have different and separate interests to protect. The new owners, unaccustomed to the nuances of working together, often disagree on how the corporation should be run and what changes are needed.

Inexperience causes additional problems. After the conversion is complete, the new owners may discover that the building requires unexpected repairs, forcing them to raise more money. It's a decided advantage if one or more of the persons in charge has been through conversions before; they can help the other new owners avoid expensive mistakes.

Even with these problems, conversions continue in high-quality buildings, offering specific advantages for many people, especially young city dwellers.

* * *

At present the advantages of condo and co-op ownership outweigh the problems, and they appear to be not only the important housing market of today, but the wave of the future. If you own either a condominium or a cooperative you have a piece of prime property.

14

Renting Your House

One wrinkle in the real estate market that's been catching on lately is for homeowners—who would, in a stronger market, be interested in selling—to rent their houses instead and hold on to the property either for income or investment.

One client of mine has for years been renting his house in a suburban community (he lives in the city) for all but his vacation time in the summer, when he and his family arrive to make use of local beaches and tennis courts. During the rest of the year, the house is rented on a long-term lease. The rent covers costs of maintenance and he gets substantial tax credits. He also gets his vacation and, in the future, a valuable property where he can retire or which he can sell.

A lawyer friend of mine, finding that real estate values in his area were rising by some 15 percent a year, bought two houses as investment property. He rents both of them on long-term leases. The rent covers maintenance, and he feels that he has a very profitable investment.

You may find that renting your house is the best alternative to selling in a difficult market. Real estate continues to be, over the long haul, a good investment. Renting your house can allow you to profit from property appreciation, while the expenses of maintaining the property are covered by the rent.

Even if you are forced to move to another area, you may want to keep your house, and if it is desirable, you may be able to draw a long-term income from the property. In any case, rental offers a viable alternative to settling for an unsatisfactory price on your property and gives you the time and leeway to find a better deal. The ins and outs of preparing a lease and renting property could be profitable information.

How to Find a Tenant

The most important factor in renting your house is to find a tenant. It is a procedure similar to finding a buyer, although it's often easier since the tenant doesn't have to make a large outlay of cash or an exceedingly long-term commitment.

People rent houses for many different reasons. First, many of them don't have enough money to buy. Downpayments are high, interest rates are up, and mortgages are hard to come by. But even for those with money, renting may be a plus. Renters have freer and more immediate access to their money. Though it may mean giving up tax savings and possible long-term gains, they keep more money available and can put it into high-yield investments.

Renters also have more freedom of movement and fewer annoyances. Even long-term leases have sublet clauses. And renters don't have to worry about maintenance inside or outside the building. For many, this alone is worth money, for they have neither the time nor the interest it takes to keep and maintain a house.

There are prospective tenants everywhere, so it's important for you to get the word out. Word of mouth, notices in stores and on community bulletin boards, and advertising in shopper's journals and local newspapers are all good first steps. Often, that's all you'll have to do.

You can also list rentals with a local real estate broker. Here, the tenant will pay any brokerage fee. There are also, in many communities, apartment-finders, who have no real estate broker's license, but carry rental listings and charge lower fees to rental tenants.

Make sure your house is ready to show. The better it looks to the prospective tenant, the higher the price you can command. But be prepared to be flexible in negotiating both the occupancy and the price. A house that is well organized, clean and neat, and equipped with the basic essentials that make life comfortable will rent much faster than one that is cluttered or looks messy.

I've always believed that renters should be as careful about choosing a house as buyers. It never helps to rush or coerce your prospect. A person who takes time to make the right choice will be a better tenant in the long run.

Renters today are very much aware of their rights. They will want to make sure the house or apartment is in good condition before they agree to rent, on the theory that it is easier to get landlords to make repairs before they move in. But remember that a prospect who seems to be overly demanding is not necessarily going to be a troublesome tenant in the future.

Choosing the Right Tenant

There are certain things that you as a landlord should look for in tenants. Always ask them to apply in person. Make out a simple application form and see how thoroughly they answer the questions. If a prospective tenant leaves many spaces blank, ask for more information and check references carefully. Once you accept an application, you should generally

139

hold the apartment or house while you are checking the references.

Most landlords follow guidelines of income and credit references when they choose tenants. His or her past rental record and employment history will by your two most important criteria.

If your prospective tenant is a student, or someone with a limited job history, and/or no credit record, you can ask the person to have a friend or relative co-sign the lease. Using a co-signer helps those who may not have enough references and gives you some additional protection.

What to Charge

There are a number of factors that affect your rental price: the size of your house and amenities such as a swimming pool or tennis courts. How far it is to the beach or to town, the availability of sports and amusement facilities, schools, churches, and shopping. How near the house is to rail transportation and highways. The value of furniture and furnishings, and anything that makes your house inviting, comfortable, and desirable.

To find out what a fair rental for your house would be, look at the rental listings in your local newspaper. They will give you the best idea of the rents being charged for various types and sizes of apartments.

Don't forget to consider all the extras, whether you include them in the rent or not: trash collection, recreational memberships, water and sewer taxes, utilities, insurance, and maintenance.

Rental Procedures

Once you have found a tenant there are two important steps to follow:

1. Take a deposit. As for 10 percent of the total rent, or one or two months' rent. Local law often regulates how a deposit is held or how it is to be refunded. These laws may cover items such as interest, amount of time before you must return deposit, and money damages to tenant for improper withholding.

2. Ask for letters of recommendation and bank references.

Discuss fully with the tenant the terms of tenancy. From this discussion you will make a written agreement that provides the basis for the formal lease. You want to include these basic statements:

1. The exact terms and conditions of the lease—the length of time: six months, one year, or two. And spell out any penalty for overstaying the termination of the lease.

2. The responsibility for utilities, care of grounds, repairs to appliances, fire, and structural damage.

3. A notice of renewal if there is an option to renew.

4. The way that rent will be paid—where, to whom, escrow deposit for damages, and payments in advance.

5. The responsibility for garbage collection.

6. An inventory of contents, if the house is furnished.

7. The right to sublet if the tenant feels he or she might not wish to occupy the house for the entire term of the lease.

These are the basic clauses in most leases. When you have agreed to all the terms, the next step is to prepare the actual lease.

The Lease

A lease is a written and dated legal document that records the contract between the owner and the renter. This lease, often a preprinted form, sets out all the points of agreement and includes any other conditions binding on both parties.

The renter agrees to abide by the conditions written in the lease for that period. In exchange for prompt payment of rent and the performance of the conditions, you give him or her possession of the dwelling. If the tenant defaults before the end of the lease term (when you have performed properly), he or she can be held legally responsible for the remainder of the lease term if the unit is not rerented.

Sometimes a *written agreement* is substituted for a formal lease. This is a somewhat shorter, more informal document. It often permits month-to-month occupancy and allows you to write in your own preferences. The tenant may also add or subtract provisions to an agreement. Both of you should initial all changes. This kind of agreement also permits landlords to change the rent at their discretion. Remember that some areas have rent controls. Check with local authorities to see if rent controls affect your area.

Most often a formal lease is the best of rental arrangements because it leaves no room for any misunderstanding about occupancy.

The Details

In addition to the basic statements in a lease, all leases should contain certain formal details:

A property description
Length of lease
Name of the landlord and tenant

142

Due date for rent

Amount of rent and any "late charges" associated with late
   payments of rent

Responsibilities for maintenance of the dwelling unit

Notice of requirements when terminating a lease

The tenant's rights and responsibilities

Sublease provision

Security deposit

Utilities

Laundry and recreational facilities

The landlord's rules and regulations

Signing the Lease

All parties to the lease must sign, and the signatures should be
witnessed by a disinterested party.

Both the lessor and lessee must receive signed copies of the
lease.

In any dispute, what is written and signed will be binding
upon all parties.

After the Tenant Moves In

Whenever possible, you might visit your tenants, but don't in-
vade their privacy. Keep an eye on your house if possible, but
be aware that very few people will take care of your property
the way you do. On the other hand, whenever there is a profit
there is a risk. You must expect fair wear and tear. Your escrow account should be ample to cover reasonable damages.
When a justifiable request for repairs is made, have it done
quickly. A happy tenant will look out for your property—a
disgruntled one will cause you heartache and expense.

A lived-in house never deteriorates in the same way as an

143

empty one. Having people live in your house will keep it alive and bring you a profit.

Rules and Regulations

As the landlord, you have the right to set reasonable rules and regulations for your rental property. These rules should be designed for everyone's convenience and safety, or to govern the use of shared services and utilities, such as laundry rooms, storage areas, swimming pools, or parking areas—and to preserve the property.

The regulations you set should apply to everyone occupying the premises in a fair and nondiscriminatory manner. They must be clearly stated. They legally cannot create a loophole for you to evade obligations. And you must give tenants notice of the regulations when they enter into the rental arrangement.

Most of these rules and restrictions are concerned with house parties, noise, stereos, TV or musical instruments, mounting pictures on the walls, painting or papering walls, parking spaces for tenants and guests, pets, recreation and common-use facilities, special furniture and appliances such as waterbeds and hot plates, using the grounds for outdoor activities such as games, gardening, bicycles and just hanging around, and the use of oil heaters.

Your Right of Entry

The landlord has certain basic rights—primarily the right to rent or sell the property and to collect payment when the property is rented; the right to evict or terminate renter's occupancy under certain circumstances; and the right of entry or access to the unit.

A right of entry to access is a legal term which means the tenant has given the landlord advance permission to enter the dwelling to make repairs, improvements, or provide agreed-upon services. You may also need entry to show the unit to prospective buyers, lenders, tenants, workmen, or contractors. You should come at reasonable hours, at the convenience of the tenant, except in an emergency.

Unlawful Provisions in a Lease

Some leases may contain provisions that are generally forbidden by law. For example:

- A provision that forces the tenant to agree to accept the blame in any future dispute. Such a clause will usually stipulate that he or she pay your legal fees in any court action.
- A provision permitting you to exert unfair leverage on the tenant such as collecting, then failing to return deposits under false pretenses.
- A provision permitting you to assume possession of the tenant's personal property for failure to pay rent.
- A provision freeing you from responsibility for negligence if the tenant or his or her guests are injured on the premises.
- A provision permitting action against the tenant by eviction, shutting off the water, padlocking doors, and turning off the heat for things such as organizing a tenants' union, complaining to proper authorities about housing code violations, or making do-it-yourself repairs.
- A provision permitting the landlord to force the tenant to continue to pay rent for a dwelling gutted by fire, tornado, or other disaster.

145

Renting Out Your Second Home

About 3 million homeowners in the United States have some kind of second home. At one time, vacation homes offered a tremendous tax advantage. It was a popular money game to buy vacation houses to increase tax losses and offset other income. But the Tax Reform Act of 1976 changed the rules of the game.

The new law now lets you claim full tax benefits on the rental of a vacation home only if you limit your own personal use of the house to fourteen days each taxable year. Even with this restriction, a vacation house is still a valuable investment for people in a high-income and high-tax bracket.

If you use the house for less than two weeks a year, you can deduct maintenance, depreciation, furniture, the expense of traveling between your first and second home for inspection purposes, and any commissions paid to a rental agent. All of these deductions are in addition to the standard deduction of mortgage interest and property taxes.

However, if you use the vacation home more than fourteen days—or more than 10 percent of the number of rental days, whichever is greater—you can claim only interest paid on mortgage payments and property taxes.

There is still some confusion about the new laws governing vacation homes and tax allowances; a tax counselor can tell you if renting out your second home will give you a valuable tax shelter.

A vacation home in a desirable location can be an excellent investment if you have some money set aside and are in a high-tax bracket. It is a good way to generate an estate or protect savings against the drain of inflation. A resort home can be written off over the years so that it actually pays for itself.

Later, you can live there, in a home that literally cost you nothing to buy.

Newly built second homes can be depreciated at a higher rate than used homes, and so offer a greater tax savings. Under IRS guidelines the allowable depreciation on a new house is 8 percent, compared to 5 percent for a used one. At the same time, a house in a quality area steadily appreciates in value because of inflation.

It is also possible to make some money out of a vacation home by taking only the standard deductions of mortgage interest and property taxes. If you want to use your second house more than two weeks each year, choose one in a highly desirable area. You can then rent it for the prime season—usually winter or summer—at an extremely high rent. You probably won't make enough money to cover the full cost of ownership, but it will help offset some of your expenses.

If you are considering this kind of second house, choose one in a location that you can enjoy in months other than the prime season.

Some Problems

A second home that you buy to rent carries some inherent problems. Location is everything. To attract tenants willing to pay a high monthly or seasonal rent, it has to be in a sought-after living or resort area, ideally one that has year-round attractions. There are few such locations, and they are usually expensive. But it is the only way the investment will pay off.

The basic problem with all rentals is the tenants. You will have to choose them carefully, especially if you rent the house month to month. A careless tenant can destroy your profit in a week's time. Check credentials, employment records, and previous landlords. If you rent regularly, you will eventually gain a certain kind of instinct about tenants.

Even the best of them will have maintenance problems from time to time and will expect you to cope. Pipes freeze and burst in ski houses; roofs leak; sudden storms break windows at beach houses. A tenant in a vacation house for a couple of weeks or months is going to need assistance. Put in writing the kinds of repairs and maintenance for which you will be responsible, and those that the tenant should take care of.

It's a good idea to keep a cash reserve equal to at least three months' rent as protection against unforeseen expenses on your vacation house. Increases in property taxes, higher energy costs, and unexpected repairs can suddenly deplete your bank account. There may also be some months when you are unable to rent the house.

A second house is a long-term investment. You cannot make a profit by buying and selling within a year or two. But if you're in the right kind of income bracket, it is an outstanding investment.

A standard house lease, spelling out the rights and duties of both landlord and tenant, is available from most office supply and stationery stores.

15

The Last Resort
(If You Go to a Broker)

Throughout this book I've tried to show you how to handle the sale of your house without using a broker and without paying a broker's commission. I've tried to pass along the know-how of many years' experience in real estate and some of the feints and inside moves picked up during a lifetime in that industry.

Even with this inside information, it is possible that you won't be able to sell your own house for a reasonable profit. There can be a number of reasons for this.

• You may be too emotionally involved with the house to successfully negotiate a sale;

• You may have gotten stuck at an unrealistic price and find yourself unable to move off it, despite the evidence;

• You may not have the time to do a proper job of selling the house;

• You may not have the time to stick with a difficult sale and see the number of prospects necessary;

• You may too readily reveal your home's weak points and discourage possible buyers;

• You may incorrectly judge possible buyers and spend your available time dealing with persons who have no chance to get a mortgage or meet your price.

In today's real estate market it is crucial for a seller to understand mortgages. Your selling price partly includes selling a good, quality mortgage. If creative financing—a necessity in most sales today—is mind-boggling for you, a broker can be invaluable.

What a Broker Does

Quite often, we earn our money. During the course of an average day, I may travel a hundred miles, examine a dozen houses, talk with more than a score of people. I spend at least a few hours every week with bankers, discussing various methods of financing and occasionally negotiating a loan for a prospective buyer.

Most mornings I spend with real estate advertisements—reading them for information, learning how to make my own ads better, writing new ones. I keep in constant touch with what's on the market, looking at available houses, sizing them up, evaluating and re-evaluating the market, and re-evaluating the properties that I'm handling.

The heart of any day is the time I pass with prospective buyers—matching them with the house that best fits their needs, negotiating between them and the person I basically work for: the homeowner, looking for a way to make a deal that will satisfy the requirements of all parties. When I make a deal, I know that I've earned the commission, because I don't just list a lot of houses and sit back waiting for buyers to beat a path to my door.

I concentrate on relatively few properties and apply my knowledge and effort to selling these, using the sort of information I've tried to pass on to you. It's an approach that's been successful for me and should work for you.

But there are no certainties, and you may not be able to successfully handle your own real estate deal either for the reasons I've already mentioned, or for some other reason. Market conditions over which you have no control, for instance.

So you should have some idea of what you want a broker to do for you, how best to deal with your broker, and get him or her to do the best possible job for his employer—you.

A state licensed real estate broker (as opposed to an agent who may work for a broker) should be a professional who spends his or her full time working in the business. A broker has a minimum of two years' experience in real estate and works primarily for himself or herself. An agent, on the other hand, always hangs out a license with a broker. A part-time real estate agent will probably not give you the sort of attention you need.

To begin with, a good real estate broker provides a clearing center for houses on the market. If you have had trouble setting a realistic price on your house, the broker can help you. Sit down with him or her and go through the multiple-listing service. This should give you a good understanding of the available houses and price ranges in specific areas. This is one of the most important areas of agreement between you and the broker. If the two of you cannot reach a common figure that you find acceptable, go to another one. If you cannot reach the right figure with any of the brokers you visit, your expectations are probably unrealistic and you should rethink the entire proposition.

Generally a broker acts as a negotiating party between you and the buyer, but he or she is working primarily for you. If you have found it difficult to negotiate directly, his services as arbiter can be invaluable.

Although you are the principal client, the broker should also actively cooperate with the buyer, for your broker can often help the buyer find a way to purchase your house. He or she can provide general information about a community and specific information about schools and businesses. Sometimes brokers can actively assist a buyer in obtaining financing, but you cannot count on this.

In general, a buyer should be able to do business with either a reputable broker or an owner. But insofar as the buyer is concerned, a broker has certain built-in advantages. For example, not being emotionally involved, the broker can be an advocate for the seller and yet not be blind to the shortcomings of a particular property. And, a large part of a broker's success is based on salesmanship. This doesn't mean pushing or forcing a property on someone, but directing the client to a positive point of view. Buyers, almost by definition, will settle on negatives. It's the broker's job to keep the focus positive.

For example, I recently handled a fine three-bedroom home in a suburban development. All of the back windows and sliding glass patio doors gave out onto a superb view of a lake with distant hills visible behind it. However, directly behind the house was a vacant lot. The lot had been empty for five years and there were no immediate plans that I knew of for a house to go up on it, thereby blocking the view of the house I was selling. Even so, I did not emphasize the view as a selling point.

The owner wanted to describe the view in an ad and I discouraged him from doing so. The reason? As mentioned, buyers always look at the negative side. If you promote a selling point and there is any flaw in it, a prospect will immediately pick it up. If we had advertised the view as a plus, any client would immediately say, upon entering the house, "Yes, but what happens when they build on that empty lot?"

This selecting of selling points and balancing them with a realistic appraisal of the house is a fairly subtle process. Some people have a natural instinct for it, others learn from experience. It is a major function of a broker and a quality you should look for if you decide to choose a broker for your house.

The broker should be skilled at negotiating and should be able to convince you that the price he or she sets gives you the fair market value and a reasonable profit, while also being able to convince the buyer that he is getting the best of all possible deals. This is the reason why 60 percent of all home sales are conducted by brokers.

When you sell your house through a broker, you usually add an extra amount to its base price to make up for the commission. A commission is usually 6 to 7 percent of the sales price, but it may be negotiable, depending on the services you require.

While this percentage may seem high, many sellers are not aware that the commission is frequently split between a broker and a sales or listing agent, and sometimes among all three.

For example, if an agent sells a home for $100,000, the 6 percent commission is $6,000. The selling agent receives half the commission, which he usually must split with a listing agent—two agents receiving $1,500 each. The broker receives $3,000.

If a broker sells his own listing on $100,000, the result is $6,000. Because a broker generally receives a larger commission, he or she is generally more flexible in negotiating and might be willing to throw percentage points in to put the sale together.

If the listing and selling agent are one, the commission can be negotiated with a little more ease. But if a broker does both ends, you've both got more room to bargain.

Competitive conditions in the marketplace as well as a serious concern over inflation have encouraged a number of sellers and brokers to look for other means of marketing a house without paying the full brokerage fee. People are recognizing that if they hire a broker to sell their home, they should be able to negotiate fees in the same way as they might with any other professional.

One method that seems to be finding favor is to request that a house be listed on a dual-fee system. This calls for a lower fee if the broker who lists the property finds the buyer himself, and a full fee if the house is sold by another broker who shares in the fee.

It is also possible for you to ask for an open listing which means being listed with a number of individual brokers and even retaining an option to sell the house yourself.

Under another new plan, one broker has been experimenting with a three-way option. The broker lists the house, and if it sells through normal multiple-listing channels, he receives a standard 7 percent commission at the time of the sale. If, however, the house is purchased by a buyer who has agreed in advance to pay the broker as a buyer-broker, then there is no charge to the seller and a 5 percent charge to the buyer. If the seller finds a buyer himself during the listing period, he pays a flat fee of $1,000 to the broker.

If you decide to place your house on the market with a broker, you should first see what the broker's attitude is toward the sale. Is he more interested in getting an exclusive right to sell than in selling the house?

What to Look For

Make sure that the broker is doing a proper job for you.
- Is the broker advertising your house? If not, you have a legitimate complaint.
- Does the broker thoroughly screen prospective buyers?
- Has he thoroughly explained the pricing of your house to you?

- Is he really trying to sell the house or merely showing it?
- Has he posted a FOR SALE sign on your property?
- Is he willing to accept a qualified buyer from another broker and split the commission?

Check and find out the price he or she is quoting to prospective buyers.

- Does he tell you about the results after showing your house?
- Does he tell you what prospective buyers have to say?
- If he asks you to accept a low offer, will he accept a reduced commission?
- Finally, how often does your broker communicate with you? Are the lines of communication open? Do you feel free to bring up any ideas or ask any questions that you don't understand about pending deals?

You might ask yourself, if you were the buyer, would you want to buy from this broker or agent? Does the person come across as fair, honest, equitable, committed, knowledgeable, and concerned? These are qualities that you have a right to expect.

Glossary of Real Estate Terms

This glossary includes words and terms commonly used in real estate transactions. However, state laws, as well as custom and interpretation in various parts of the country, may modify or change some of the meanings. Before signing any documents or depositing money preparatory to entering into a real estate contract, always consult an attorney to be sure your rights are protected. *Note:* Italicized words within a definition are defined elsewhere in the alphabetical listing.

Abstract (Of Title). A summary of public records relating to the *title* to a particlar piece of land. An attorney or *title insurance* company reviews an abstract of title to determine whether there are any title defects that must be cleared before a buyer can purchase clear, *marketable title* and insurable title.

Acceleration Clause. A condition in a *mortgage* that may require the balance of the loan to become due immediately if regular mortgage payments are not made or for breach of other conditions of the mortgage.

Agreement of Sale. A contract in which a seller agrees to sell and a buyer agrees to buy, under certain specific terms and conditions spelled out in writing and signed by both parties. According to location or jurisdiction, an agreement of sale may also be known as contract of purchase, purchase agreement, or sales agreement.

Amortization. A payment plan that enables the borrower to reduce his or her debt gradually through monthly payments of *principal*.

Appraisal. An expert judgment or estimate of the quality or value of real estate as of a given date.

Assumption of Mortgage. An obligation by the buyer to be personally liable for payment of an existing *mortgage*. In an assumption, the purchaser is substituted for the original *mortgagor* in the mortgage instrument and the original mortgagor is released from further liability. The *mortgagee's* consent is usually required.

To be fully released under the assumption, the original mortgagor should always obtain a written release from further liability. Failure to obtain such a release renders the original mortgagor liable if the new buyer fails to make the monthly payments.

An assumption of mortgage is often confused with "purchasing subject to a mortgage." Here, the buyer also agrees to make the monthly mortgage payments on an existing mortgage. But if the buyer fails to make the payments, the original mortgagor remains personally liable. In this situation, the mortgagee's consent is not required.

Both assumption of mortgage and purchasing subject to a mortgage are used to finance the sale of property. They may also be used when a mortgagor is in financial difficulty and desires to sell the property to avoid *foreclosure*.

Binder or Offer to Purchase. A preliminary agreement, secured by the payment of *earnest money,* between a buyer and seller as an offer to purchase real estate. A binder secures the right to purchase for a limited period of time. If the buyer changes his or her mind or is unable to purchase, the earnest money is forfeited unless the binder expressly provides that it is to be refunded.

Building Line or Setback. Distances from the ends and/or sides of the lot beyond which construction may not extend. The building line may be established by a filed *plat* of subdivision, by *restrictive covenants* in *deeds* or leases, by building codes, or by *zoning ordinances*.

Caveat. A warning or notice to take heed such as a clause in a document which is meant to be a warning.

Certificate of Title. A certificate issued by a *title* company or a written opinion rendered by an attorney that the seller has good marketable and insurable title to the property which is offered for sale. A certificate of title offers no protection against any hidden defects in the title which an examination of the records could not reveal. The issuer of a certificate of title is liable only for damages due to negligence. The protection offered a homeowner under a certificate of title is not as great as that offered in a *title insurance* policy.

Closing Costs. Sometimes called settlement costs. The numerous expenses which buyers and sellers normally incur to complete a transaction in the transfer of ownership of real estate. These costs are in addition to the price of the property and are prepaid on the *closing day.*

The *agreement of sale* negotiated previously between the buyer and seller should state in writing who will pay what costs. The buyer usually pays for appraisal and inspection, attorney's fee, documentary stamps on notes, escrow fees, recording deed and mortgage, survey charge, and title insurance. The seller usually pays for his own attorney's fee, cost of abstract, documentary stamps on deed, and real estate commission.

Closing Day. Date of actual transfer of ownership of real property. The *certificate of title, abstract,* and *deed* are generally prepared for the closing day by an attorney and this cost charged to the buyer. The buyer signs the mortgage, and closing costs are paid. The final closing merely confirms the original agreement reached in the *agreement of sale.*

Cloud (On Title). An outstanding claim or encumbrance which adversely affects the marketability of title.

Commission. Money paid to a real estate agent or broker by the seller as compensation for finding a buyer and completing the sale. Usually it is a percentage of the sale price—6 to 7 percent on houses, 10 percent on land.

Condemnation. The taking of private property for public use by a government unit, against the will of the owner, but with payment of just compensation under the government's power of eminent domain. A

159

governmental agency may also condemn a particular building as unsafe or unfit for use.

Condominium. Individual ownership of a dwelling unit and an individual interest in the common areas and facilities which serve the multiunit project.

Contingency. One or more conditions that must be met before the contract becomes binding.

Contract of Purchase. See *Agreement of sale.*

Contractor. A contractor is one who erects buildings or portions of them. There are also contractors for each phase of construction: heating, electricity, plumbing, air conditioning, road building, bridge and dam erection, and others.

Conventional Mortgage. A *mortgage* loan is subject to conditions established by the lending institutions and state statutes. The mortgage rates may vary with different institutions and between states. A conventional mortgage is not insured by HUD or guaranteed by the Veterans Administration.

Convey. To transfer title from one person to another.

Cooperative Housing. An apartment building or a group of dwellings owned by a corporation, the stockholders of which are residents of the dwellings. It is operated by their elected board of directors. The corporation or association owns title to the real estate. A resident purchases stock in the corporation which entitles him or her to occupy a unit in the building or property. The resident does not own the unit but has an absolute right to occupy it for as long as he owns the stock.

Covenant. A promise usually in the form of a recorded agreement when used as a part of the language of real estate.

Deed. A formal written instrument by which *title* to real property is transferred from one owner to another. The deed, which should contain an accurate description of the property, must be signed and witnessed according to the laws of the state where the property is located, and should be delivered to the buyer at *closing day.* There are two parties to the deed: the *grantor* and the *grantee.* (See also: *deed of trust, general warranty deed, quitclaim deed,* and *special warranty deed.*)

Deed of Trust. Like a mortgage, a security instrument whereby real property is given as security for a debt. However, in a deed of trust, there are three parties to the instrument: the borrower, the *trustee,* and the lender (or beneficiary). The borrower transfers the legal *title* for the property to the trustee, who holds it as security for payment of debt to the lender. When the borrower pays the debt as agreed, the deed of trust becomes void. If, however, he or she *defaults,* the trustee may sell the property at a public sale, under the terms of the deed of trust. In most jurisdictions where the deed of trust is in force, the borrower may have his or her property sold without legal proceedings. In recent years some states have begun to treat the deed of trust like a *mortgage.*

Default. Failure to make mortgage payments as agreed in the mortgage or deed of trust. It is the mortgagor's responsibility to remember the due date and send the payment prior to the due date, not after. Generally, if payment is not received thirty days after the due date, the mortgage is in default. The mortgage may give the lender the right to accelerate payments, take possession and receive rents, and start *foreclosure.* Defaults may also come about by the failure to observe other conditions in the mortgage or deed of trust.

Depreciation. Decline in value of a house because of wear and tear, adverse changes in the neighborhood, or any other reason.

Documentary Stamps. A state tax, in the form of stamps, required on *deeds* and *mortgages* when real estate *title* passes from one owner to another. The amount of stamps required varies with each state.

Downpayment. Money paid by the buyer to the seller when the *agreement of sale* is signed. The agreement of sale specifies the amount and acknowledges receipt of the downpayment. Downpayment is the difference between the sales price and the maximum mortgage amount. If the buyer fails to buy the property without good cause, the downpayment is not always refundable. If the buyer wants the downpayment to be refundable he or she should insert a clause in the agreement of sale specifying the conditions under which the deposit will be refunded. If the seller cannot deliver good *title,* the agreement of sale usually requires the seller to return the downpayment and to pay interest and expenses incurred by the purchaser.

Earnest Money. The deposit money given to the seller or his or her agent by the potential buyer to show that he is serious about buying the house. If the sale goes through, the earnest money is applied against the *downpayment.* If the sales does not go through, the earnest money will be forfeited or lost unless the *binder* or *offer to purchase* expressly provides that it is refundable.

Easement Rights. A right-of-way granted to a person or company authorizing access to or over the owner's land. For example, a power company's obtaining a right-of-way across private property.

Encroachment. An obstruction, building, or part of a building that intrudes beyond a legal boundary onto neighboring land, or a building extending beyond the *building line.*

Encumbrance. A legal right or interest in land that affects a good or clear title and diminishes the land's value. It can take numerous forms, such as *zoning ordinances, easement rights,* claims, *mortgages, liens,* charges, a pending legal action, unpaid *taxes,* or *restrictive covenants.* An encumbrance does not legally prevent transfer of the property to another. A *title search* usually reveals the existence of such encumbrances, and it is up to the buyer to determine whether he or she wants to purchase with the encumbrance, or what can be done to remove it.

Equity. The value of a homeowner's unencumbered interest in real estate. Equity is computed by subtracting from the property's fair market value the total of the unpaid mortgage balance and any outstanding liens or other debts against the property. A homeowner's equity increases as he or she pays off the mortgage or as the property appreciates in value. When the mortgage and all other debts against the property are paid in full, the homeowner has 100 percent equity.

Escrow. Documents or monies held, generally by a third party, until all conditions and contingencies have been met.

In FHA mortgage transactions an escrow account usually refers to the funds a mortgagor pays the lender at the time of the mortgage payments. The money is held in a trust fund provided by the lender. Such funds cover yearly expenditures for *mortgage insurance premiums,* taxes, *hazard insurance* premiums, and *special assessments.*

Evaluation. An educated determination based upon historical data, and experience of the fair market value of a property compared to all other properties of like value.

Foreclosure. A legal term applied to various methods of enforcing payment of the debt secured by a *mortgage,* or *deed of trust,* by taking and selling the mortgaged property.

General Warranty Deed. A deed that conveys all the *grantor's* interests in and title to the property to the *grantee,* and also warrants that if the title is defective or has a *cloud* on it the grantee may hold the grantor liable.

Grantee. That party in the *deed* who is the buyer or recipient.

Grantor. That party in the *deed* who is the seller or giver.

Hazard Insurance. Protects against damages caused to property by fire, windstorms, and other common hazards.

HUD. U.S. Department of Housing and Urban Development. The Office of Housing/Federal Housing Administration within HUD insures home mortgage loans and sets minimum standards for such homes.

Lien. A claim by one person on the property of another as security for money owed. Such claims may include obligations not met or satisfied, judgments, unpaid taxes, materials, or labor. (See also *special lien.*)

Listing. A written agreement between a broker and an owner to sell or lease real property.

Marketable Title. A *title* that is free and clear of objectionable *liens, clouds,* or other title defects. A title which enables an owner to sell his or her property freely to others and which others will accept without objection.

Market Value. The highest price that a buyer without duress is ready, willing and able to pay, and the lowest price a seller is ready, willing and able to accept.

Mortgage. A *lien* or claim against real property given by the buyer to the lender as security for money borrowed. Under government-insured or loan-guaranteed provisions, the payments may include *escrow* amounts covering taxes, *hazard insurance,* water charges, and *special*

163

assessments. Mortgages generally run from ten to thirty years, during which the loan is to be paid off.

Mortgage Commitment. A written notice from the bank or other lending institution saying it will advance mortgage funds in a specified amount to enable a buyer to purchase a house.

Mortgagee. The lender in a mortgage agreement.

Mortgage Insurance Premium. The payment made by a borrower to the lender for transmittal to HUD to help defray the cost of the FHA mortgage insurance program and to provide a reserve fund to protect lenders against loss in insured mortgage transactions. In FHA-insured mortgages this represents an annual rate of one-half of one percent paid by the mortgagor on a monthly basis.

Mortgage Note. A written agreement to repay a loan. The agreement secured by a *mortgage* serves as proof of an indebtedness and states the manner in which it shall be paid. The note states the actual amount of the debt that the mortgage secures and renders the *mortgagor* personally responsible for repayment.

Mortgage (Open End). A mortgage with a provision that permits borrowing additional money in the future without *refinancing* the loan or paying additional financing charges. Open-end provisions often limit such borrowing to no more than would raise the balance to the original loan figure.

Mortgagor. The borrower in a mortgage agreement.

Plat. A map or chart of a lot, subdivision, or community drawn by a surveyor showing boundary lines, buildings, improvements on the land, and *easements.*

Points. Sometimes called "discount points." A point is one percent of the amount of the mortgage loan. For example, if a loan is for $25,000, one point is $250. Points are charged by a lender to raise the yield on the loan at a time when money is tight, interest rates are high, and there is a legal limit to the interest rate that can be charged on a mortgage. Buyers are prohibited from paying points on HUD- or VA-guaranteed loans (sellers can pay, however). On a *conventional* mortgage, points may be paid by either buyer or seller or split between them.

Prepayment. Payment of mortgage loan, or part of it, before due date. Mortgage agreements often restrict the right of prepayment either by limiting the amount that can be prepaid in any one year or charging a penalty for prepayment. The FHA does not permit such restrictions in FHA-insured mortgages.

Principal. The basic element of the loan as distinguished from *interest* and *mortgage insurance* premium. In other words, principal is the amount upon which interest is paid.

Purchase Agreement. See *Agreement of sale.*

Quitclaim Deed. A deed which transfers whatever interest the maker of the deed may have in the property. A quitclaim deed is often given to clear the title when the grantor's interest in a property is questionable. The buyer assumes all the risks. Such a deed makes no warranties as to the title, but simply transfers to the buyer whatever interest the grantor has.

Real Estate Broker. A middleman or agent who buys and sells real estate for a company, firm, or individual on a *commission* basis. The broker does not have title to the property, but generally represents the owner.

Refinancing. The process of the same mortgagor paying off one loan with the proceeds from another loan.

Restrictive Covenants. Private restrictions limiting the use of real property. Restrictive covenants are created by *deed* and may "run with the land," binding all subsequent purchases of the land, or may be "personal" and binding only between the original seller and buyer. The determination whether a covenant runs with the land or is personal is governed by the language of the covenant, the intent of the parties, and the law in the state where the land is situated.

Restrictive covenants that run with the land are *encumbrances* and may affect the value and marketability of *title.* Restrictive covenants may limit the density of buildings per acre, regulate size, style, or price range of buildings to be erected, or prevent particular businesses from operating or minority groups from owning or occupying homes in a given area. (This last covenant is unconstitutional and has been declared unenforceable by the U.S. Supreme Court.)

Sales Agreement. See *Agreement of sale.*

Special Assessments. A special tax imposed on property, individual lots or all property in the immediate area for road construction, sidewalks, sewers, street lights, etc.

Special Lien. A lien that binds a specified piece of property, unlike a general *lien,* which is levied against all one's assets. It creates a right to retain something of value belonging to another person as compensation for labor, material, or money expended in that person's behalf. In some localities it is called "particular" lien or "specific" lien. (See *lien.*)

Special Warranty Deed. In a special warranty deed the grantor guarantees that he or she has done nothing while holding title to the property which has impaired, or which might in the future impair, the grantee's title.

State Stamps. See *Documentary stamps.*

Survey. A map or *plat* made by a licensed surveyor showing the measurements of the land with its elevations, improvements, boundaries, and its relationship to surrounding tracts of land. A survey is often required to assure the lender that a building is actually sited on the land according to its legal description.

Tax. As applied to real estate, an enforced charged imposed on persons, property, or income, to be used to support the state.

Title. Generally, the rights of ownership and possession of particular property. In real estate usage, title may refer to the instruments or documents by which a right of ownership is established (title documents), or it may refer to the ownership interest one has in the real estate.

Title Insurance. Protects lenders or homeowners against loss of their interest in property due to legal defects in title. Title insurance may be issued to either the *mortgagor*, as an "owner's title policy," or to the mortgagee, as a "mortgagee's title policy." Insurance benefits will be paid only to the "named insured" in the title policy. An owner must purchase an "owner's title policy," if this protection is wanted.

Title Search or Examination. A check of the *title* records, generally at the local courthouse, to make sure the buyer is purchasing a house from the legal owner and there are no liens, overdue *special assessments,* or other claims or outstanding restrictive covenants filed in the record that would adversely affect the marketability or value of title.

Trustee. A party given legal responsibility to hold property in the best interest of or "for the benefit of" another. The trustee is in a position of responsibility for another, a responsibility enforceable in a court of law. (See *deed of trust.*)

Zoning Ordinances. The acts of an authorized local government establishing building codes and setting forth regulations for property land usage.

Special Condo Language

Assessment (Operating). Proportionate share of the budgeted annual cost to maintain physically the common areas and elements of a condominium and to maintain sufficient reserves to assure financial stability. The annual assessment is reduced to monthly charges payable to the association of owners.

Assessment (Special). An assessment for some special purpose or because of inadequate budgeting of operating expenses.

Common Area or Common Estate. Generally, this encompasses all of a condominium which is not specifically delineated and described as dwelling or commercial units.

Common or Undivided Interest. Condominium association, association of owners, condominium association board of directors, or council of co-owners—the governing body of a condominium, elected by and from

167

among the owners upon conveyance of titles to the individual owner by the grantor. Its authority to operate comes from the declaration. It must operate within the framework of the bylaws.

Condominium Regime. The mode of self-rule established when condominium documents are recorded. The term also refers to all the documents necessary to legally constitute a condominium and to permit it to operate as such.

Declaration. A document which contains conditions, covenants, and restrictions governing the sale, ownership, use, and disposition of a property within the framework of applicable state condominium laws.

Delineate. To describe the physical boundaries of a dwelling unit in a condominium.

Depreciation. A decline in the value of a dwelling unit as the result of wear and tear, adverse changes in the neighborhood and its patterns, or for any other reason.

Grantor. Under a condominium regime, the owner of the property which is being subdivided into a multiple number of individual unit estates.

Latent Defect Bond. One type is an assurance required by HUD that defects due to faulty materials and workmanship found within a year of the date of completion will be corrected.

Leasehold Interest. The right to use a property under certain conditions which does not carry with it the rights of ownership.

Liability and Hazard Insurance. Insurance to protect against negligent actions of the association of owners and damages caused to property by fire, windstorm, and other common hazards.

Mortgage Loan (Individual Units). The amount lent by the lender (mortgagee) to the individual owner (mortgagor) necessary to purchase the unit.

Mortgage Loan (HUD Insured). The lender is insured by HUD against default by the mortgagor to induce the lender to lend a larger sum to the buyer. The loan limits are established by HUD.

Mortgage Loan (Project). Provides money to the builder/developer to acquire the land and construct the condominium. This loan should be paid off in full by the cash and individual mortgage loans that come into existence when all sales have been consummated. At such time the condominium individual units must be free and clear of all liens and all individual unit mortgages must be first mortgages assumed by owners of the units.

Plats and Plans. Drawings used by surveyors and architects to show the exact location of utilities, streets, buildings, and units within the buildings, in relation to the boundary lines of the total property. They may also show units, common areas, and restricted areas.

Prepaid Expenses. The initial deposit at time of closing, for taxes and subsequent monthly deposits made to the lender for that purpose. Hazard insurance is not a mortgage payment under the individual unit mortgage.

Repair and Maintenance. The costs incurred in replacing damaged items or maintaining housing systems to prevent damage. In a condominium the owner is responsible for repairing and maintaining the dwelling unit, and the condominium association is responsible for repairing and maintaining the common areas. The owner only pays his or her proportionate share of the cost to the association.

Reserve Funds (General Operating). Funds accumulated on a monthly basis to provide a cushion of capital to be used when and if a contingency arises.

Reserve Funds (Replacement). Funds set aside in *escrow* from monthly payments to replace common elements, such as roofs, at some future date.

Taxes. Local real estate assessments levied on the individual units and not on the condominium association.

Undivided Interest. In condominium law, the joint ownership of common areas in which the individual percentages are known but are not applied to separate the areas physically. This situation is similar to the joint ownership of an automobile or home by husband and wife.

Unit Value Ratio. A percentage developed by dividing the initial appraised value of a unit by the total value of all units. The percentage attaches to the dwelling unit and determines the percentage of value of the common estate attached to that unit.